how to
garden

how to
garden

gardening made easy with step-by-step techniques

jonathan edwards

HERMES
HOUSE

This edition is published by Hermes House, an imprint of
Anness Publishing Ltd, Hermes House, 88–89 Blackfriars Road,
London SE1 8HA; tel. 020 7401 2077; fax 020 7633 9499

www.hermeshouse.com; www.annesspublishing.com

If you like the images in this book and would like to investigate
using them for publishing, promotions or advertising, please visit
our website www.practicalpictures.com for more information.

Publisher: Joanna Lorenz
Managing Editor: Linda Fraser
Project Editor: Rebecca Clunes
Copy Editor: Lydia Darbyshire
Designer: Michael Morey
Editorial Reader: Penelope Goodare
Picture Research: Gary Murphy, Joanna Skordis, Nansong Lue
Production Controller: Steve Lang

ETHICAL TRADING POLICY

At Anness Publishing we believe that business should be conducted in an ethical and ecologically
sustainable way, with respect for the environment and a proper regard to the replacement of the
natural resources we employ.

As a publisher, we use a lot of wood pulp to make high-quality paper for printing, and that wood
commonly comes from spruce trees. We are therefore currently growing more than 500,000 trees in
two Scottish forest plantations near Aberdeen – Berrymoss (130 hectares/320 acres) and West
Touxhill (125 hectares/305 acres). The forests we manage contain twice the number of trees
employed each year in paper-making for our books.

Because of this ongoing ecological investment programme, you, as our customer, can have the
pleasure and reassurance of knowing that a tree is being cultivated on your behalf to naturally
replace the materials used to make the book you are holding.

Our forestry programme is run in accordance with the UK Woodland Assurance Scheme (UKWAS)
and will be certified by the internationally recognized Forest Stewardship Council (FSC). The FSC
is a non-government organization dedicated to promoting responsible management of the world's
forests. Certification ensures forests are managed in an environmentally sustainable and socially
responsible basis. For further information about this scheme, go to www.annesspublishing.com/trees

A CIP catalogue record for this book is available from the British Library.

Previously published as *Dig It*

Bracketed terms are intended for American readers.

Contents

Introduction

Most people find a garden a relaxing place, but for the gardener the pleasure is immeasurably increased. Firstly, there is the fun of deciding on a design, then the satisfaction of preparing the ground and planting, followed by the sense of achievement from the careful maintenance that keeps plants looking their best.

The appeal of gardening

In recent years, interest in gardening has mushroomed, and there has been an increasing demand for advice and information. Garden designs are becoming more imaginative, although one of the most appealing things about gardening is that you don't need any special skills or experience to start you off. Basic gardening is not only fulfilling and great fun, but is so easy to achieve that nobody is excluded. Perhaps even more important is that everyone can garden to their own level and in their own way, investing as much time and money as their own particular circumstances will allow.

This sunny border has been planted with a range of hot-coloured perennials, creating a bright, cheerful atmosphere.

Getting it right

To be an efficient gardener you need to master a few basic but very important skills, so that you can avoid mistakes and get the most from the plants in your care. Many gardening techniques are common sense, such as choosing the right plant for a particular position and knowing when to water, but other skills such as sowing a lawn or planting a pond require some knowledge and a bit of practice to get right. In this book, we guide you step-by-step through all the essential garden tasks you will need, whether creating a garden from scratch or taking care of an existing one.

How to use this book

The key to successful gardening is careful planning and preparation so that it meets both your needs and aspirations. The aim of the first section of this book is to help you to design and plan your garden, whether you have a new, empty plot or are converting an existing design. Each step is thoroughly explained, from assessing what you have and its potential to making new plans for your garden and turning them into reality.

Any garden is only as successful as the soil that sustains it. For this reason, this book includes a chapter that is dedicated to explaining exactly how to assess the soil in

A stone urn planted with white and soft purples creates a lovely calm effect. Containers require a lot of watering but they do add an extra dimension to the garden.

Magnolia x *soulangeana* 'Amabilis' is a magnificent sight in mid-spring.

Columbines can be grown in the open border, but are frequently found in open woodland in the wild. Follow nature and grow them in shady borders or under a tree.

your garden, the various steps you can take to improve it, and how to prepare the ground ready for planting.

The book looks in depth at particular areas of the garden that have techniques specific to them, including lawns and water and rock gardens, using practical step sequences to help you create a successful garden. So, whether you are planning to lay or sow a new lawn from scratch or wish to renovate an old lawn, you will find all the practical answers here. Water brings an added dimension to any garden, and the section on rock and water gardening shows how to build a pond or a water feature. There is also useful information on creating a bog garden.

Many fundamental techniques apply to most if not all the areas of the garden. They are brought together in one section covering all the basics from choosing an essential tool kit, to weeding, mulching, feeding and watering as well as pest and disease control.

Finally, there is a seasonal checklist to remind you to carry out the essential tasks in all areas of the garden at the right time.

This book contains over 45 step-by-step sequences to guide you through many of the more complicated gardening techniques. Throughout, there is information to help you choose the right plants for a specific situation or purpose, such as plants that will thrive in a bog garden or that will make good ground cover and suppress weeds. Both beginners and experienced gardeners will find this book the ideal reference guide to achieve the garden they want.

Busy herbaceous borders full of strongly growing plants help to keep the weeds down, and so require less maintenance. A planting scheme like this is unbeatable in midsummer.

Planning your garden

Gardening is much more than just growing plants. To make a garden appealing, it is just as important that the setting in which the plants are placed is right. You can have your garden designed and constructed by professionals, but it will cost a great deal and the chances are that it won't give you as much satisfaction as creating a garden by your own efforts.

Only you can decide what is best for your garden. Tastes in gardens vary enormously, and the best test of a new design is whether it pleases you. Use the planning techniques suggested to experiment on paper — you will soon develop the skills that will enable you to design your garden with confidence. A well-thought-out design will ensure you make the best use of your space, and planning it is an enjoyable challenge in itself.

A well-planned garden will have points of interest all year round. Here, a border of brightly coloured tulips is a welcome sight in spring.

Assessing your garden

Whether you have the blank canvas of a new garden or are trying to make improvements to an existing design, the first step is to decide exactly what you want as well as what changes you will have to make to achieve your ideal garden.

What do you want?

This may seem a simple question, but in practice it can prove problematic, especially if there are two gardeners in the house. The easiest way to decide what you really want is to make several lists. Write down all the things in the existing garden that cannot be changed, such as the position of an established tree or a pond, as well as other features you want to keep. Then make a list of everything you really

A greenhouse takes up a lot of space in a small garden, so consider whether the use you make of it would make it worthwhile.

Garden priorities

Wish list	Essential	Desirable
Structural features		
1. Paving/decking	[ ]	[ ]
2. Gravel area	[ ]	[ ]
3. Lawn	[ ]	[ ]
4. Pond/water course	[ ]	[ ]
5. Summerhouse	[ ]	[ ]
6. Tool shed	[ ]	[ ]
7. Greenhouse	[ ]	[ ]
8. Vegetable garden	[ ]	[ ]
Utility features		
1. Washing line	[ ]	[ ]
2. Compost heap	[ ]	[ ]
3. Cold frame	[ ]	[ ]
4. Dustbin (trash) area	[ ]	[ ]
5. Built-in barbecue	[ ]	[ ]
6. Sandpit	[ ]	[ ]
7. Garden store	[ ]	[ ]
Decorative features		
1. Raised bed	[ ]	[ ]
2. Shrubbery	[ ]	[ ]
3. Herbaceous border	[ ]	[ ]
4. Wildlife area	[ ]	[ ]
5. Arch/pergola	[ ]	[ ]
6. Rock garden	[ ]	[ ]
7. Small water feature	[ ]	[ ]

want in the new design. Invariably, you will have to prioritize this "wish list" to establish which items are most important. Remember to include utility items, such as a rotary washing line or compost heap. If you find prioritizing difficult, then score each feature as either essential or desirable. In this way you can be sure to include all the essential features as well as some of the desirable ones if there is the space.

HOW TO MEASURE

Use a 3m (10ft) retractable tape measure and pegs to measure a small area. For larger areas, it would be easier to hire or buy a 30m (100ft) surveyors' tape.

Measure the plot

The next step in planning a new garden or making alterations to an existing design is to assess what the current garden has to offer and to consider its limitations. The best way to do this is to draw a rough plan of the existing plot, by eye at first, on a piece of paper and record its overall dimensions.

Small rectangular gardens are very easy to measure, and sometimes the boundary can be calculated simply by counting fence panels and multiplying by the length of a fence panel and a post. In most cases, however, you will need to measure the plot with a tape measure. A long surveyors' tape measure is extremely useful. Having someone else to hold the other end of the tape will make measuring a lot easier. Note down any changes in level from side to side or down the length of the plot. Hammer in pegs at 1m (3ft) intervals, and then work out the direction and extent of the gradient, using a piece of straight timber and a spirit (carpenter's) level.

Triangulation

Sometimes it may be difficult to measure the position of a feature, such as a tree or a pond, using right angles. Triangulation is a way of fixing the position of an object in relation to the things around it.

Find two points already fixed on your plan: the corners of the house are often used. Measure the distance from each of the two points to the object. Transfer these measurements into the scale you are using on your plan. Set a pair of compasses (a compass) to each of the scale distances in turn and scribe an arc in the approximate position. When the second arc intersects the first one your point is established.

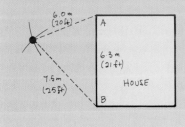

It is important to plan out a formal garden quite accurately before you start any practical work in order to get the proportions right.

HOW TO MAKE A SKETCH

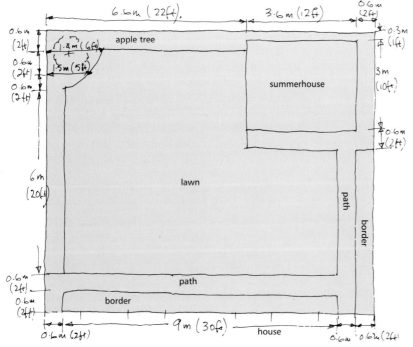

Make a rough visual sketch by eye, keeping permanent features roughly in proportion. Only include features you know you want to keep. Leave plenty of space to add measurements.

Plot the position of fixed features

Next turn your attention to the positions of permanent features, such as trees as well as other structural elements that you wish to keep in the new design. Most objects can be measured in right angles from a base line, such as the wall of the house, on your plan. If an object does not fall in a straight line from this point you will need to use triangulation (see box above left) in order to fix its position, so that it can be placed accurately on your rough sketch.

If your garden is small, sketch the whole plot in one go. If it is too big to do this, sketch it in sections that you can join together later when you draw up a scale plan.

Making plans

Drawing up an accurate plan is the best way to avoid making expensive mistakes later on. Once you have a basic plan that is drawn to scale, you can try out new ideas and see how the different elements fit together.

Draw a scale plan

Using the measurements noted down on your rough sketch of the garden, draw up a scale plan of the area being designed on graph paper, indicating the position of all the permanent features. A scale of 1:50 is suitable for most gardens (that's 2cm in the plan for every 1m in the garden, or ¼in to 1ft). However, if you are planning a large area, a scale of 1:100 (1cm per 1m or ⅛in to 1ft) may be more practical. Drawing your plan to scale will also make it easier to estimate quantities of materials, such as paving. Once you are sure they are accurate, ink the main lines in so that they show up clearly. Then, on an overlay

of acetate or tracing paper, use cross-hatching in a variety of colours to indicate areas of sun and shade at different times of the day. This information will be invaluable when you come to thinking about planting plans.

Try out new ideas

Cut out shapes from another piece of graph paper to represent the different features you want in your new garden design. You can then move the features around or alter the sizes of different elements without having to redraw the plan each time. When you are satisfied with the arrangement, draw them in position on an overlay.

Practical planning

Before ordering materials and beginning work, mark out as much of the design as possible in your existing garden. Mock up the overall shape of larger features to help you

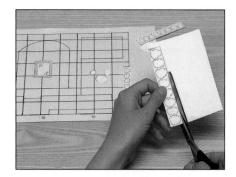

It's helpful to draw and cut out scale features that you want to include in your finished design, such as a raised pond, summerhouse or raised beds. These can be moved around until they look right, but use them as aids only. If you try to design around them, your garden will almost certainly lack coherence.

visualize the impact they will have on the rest of the garden. You could use bamboo canes as an arch or trellis, a piece of garden hose for the edge of a lawn or planks of wood to indicate the edge of a patio or path. Tall canes indicating the position of important features or key plants will

HOW TO DESIGN YOUR GARDEN

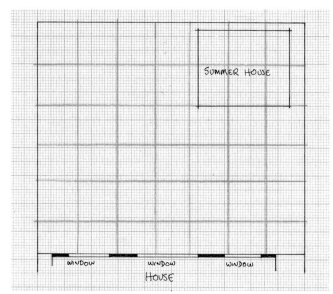

1 The basic grid Transfer all of the measurements of features you wish to retain from your first sketch on to graph paper. Superimpose on to this grid the type of design you have in mind: based on circles, diagonals or rectangles. Most gardens work best with the grid lines about 2m (7ft) apart. Using overlays or photocopies, try out features that you would like to include in their approximate positions. Moving around scale features, cut out of paper, is helpful.

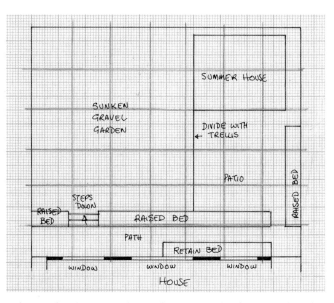

2 The rough Using an overlay or photocopies, sketch in your plan. If you can visualize an overall design, sketch this in first, then move around the cut-out features to fit. If you have not reached this stage, sketch in the features you have provisionally positioned but adjust them as the big design evolves. Make many attempts – the best plan will emerge once you have tried out lots of options. Don't worry about planning details at this stage apart from the important focal points in the design.

Getting inspired

If you are short of inspiration or cannot find a solution to a particular problem in your garden, don't be shy of being inspired by others and adapting their ideas to fit your circumstances. After all, it's what the professionals do all the time. Look at magazines and books to help decide which style appeals to you most. Also collect pictures of features that you like when you are reading magazines, and take pictures of your own when you visit other people's gardens and gardening shows. Note down any plant combinations that catch your eye; they may well come in useful later on.

DECIDING ON A PATTERN

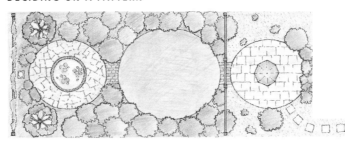

CIRCLES
A circular pattern is good at disguising the sometimes predictable shape of a rectangular garden. The circles can be overlapped, if necessary.

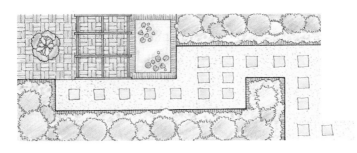

RECTANGLES
A rectangular theme is a popular choice and is effective if you want to create a formal look, or divide up a long narrow garden into smaller sections.

DIAGONALS
A diagonal grid pattern will create a sense of space by taking the eye along and across the garden. It is best to use a grid that is at 45° to the house.

show how much screening they are likely to offer. By observing the shadow at different times of day you'll also know whether shade is likely to be a problem for other plants or in a sitting-out area.

3 **The detailed drawing** Details such as the type of paving should be decided now – not only because it will help you see the final effect, but also because you need to work to a plan that uses multiples of full blocks, slabs or bricks if necessary. It will also help you to budget for your plan. Draw in key plants, especially large trees and shrubs, but omit detailed planting plans at this stage.

4 **Visualize the finished result** Before starting construction it is worth being absolutely sure what the end result will look like. If you can draw, sketch out how you plan your garden to look. You may wish to make a 3-D model of your garden, using coloured card, wooden matches and other household items, such as straw, cotton wool (cotton balls) and lentils or rice, to represent the texture of different materials. Think about the garden as it will appear at different times of the year.

Lawns and alternatives

Grass lawns have been the main feature of most domestic gardens for many years, but recent trends in garden design have provided a range of other options to consider for covering the ground.

Why choose a lawn?

A lawn is quick and easy to lay, requires little skill to maintain and looks good when it is well cared for. It is perhaps the best all-round surface and is one of the cheapest methods of covering large areas of ground. When regularly mown and trimmed, a lawn provides an attractive open space that sets off all the surrounding features and provides cohesion to the overall design. There are two main grades of domestic lawn. High quality putting- or bowling-green lawn is the most ornamental, but it requires a lot of attention and fairly frequent mowing to keep it in tip-top condition. For most people, though, a standard lawn, also called a family or utility lawn, is perfectly adequate. It is harder wearing and requires cutting less often, so it takes a lot less time to maintain. Although there are special lawn grass mixes for difficult situations, such as shade, a lawn requires more maintenance if the growing conditions are not ideal.

A lawn is one of the most important elements in a garden for many people, creating a sense of open space that lets the garden "breathe".

Lawn alternatives

In some situations such as deep shade a ground covering of shade-loving plants may be a better option. Also consider alternative coverings where mowing would be difficult or dangerous, such as on a steep slope. If you don't want a grass lawn but still require an open space in the middle of the garden, there are a number of other options you can use to cover the ground.

Herb lawns In a sunny, well-drained site a few herbs, such as camomile, thyme and comfrey, are sufficiently low growing to create a lush lawn effect. Although they are tough enough to be walked on occasionally, these plants are not hard-wearing so are not suitable for children's play areas or high-traffic walkways. Try *Thymus serpyllum* or choose the non-flowering camomile variety *Chamaemelum nobile* 'Treneague'.

HOW TO PLANT GROUND COVER PLANTS

1 Dig over the area and clear the ground of weeds at least a month before planting. Hoe off any seedlings that appear in the meantime. Rake the ground level before planting.

2 Water the plants in their pots, then set them out about 15–20cm (6–8in) apart, in staggered rows to work out the positions and to check you have sufficient plants.

3 Tease out the roots and plant to the original depth. Firm in the soil around the roots. Water thoroughly and keep well watered for the first season.

HOW TO LAY GRAVEL

1 Excavate the area to the required depth – about 5cm (2in) of gravel is sufficient in most cases. Don't disturb the soil to a greater depth than you need to.

2 Level the ground. Lay punctured, heavy-duty black polythene or a semi-permeable membrane over the area to suppress weed growth. Overlap strips by about 5cm (2in).

3 Tip the gravel on top of the base sheet and spread it evenly over the surface, making sure it is about 5cm (2in) thick. Use a rake to get the gravel level.

Ground cover plants Choose easy-care plants – low-growing conifers and heathers as well as the rose of Sharon (*Hypericum calycinum*), for example – to cover difficult or dangerous areas, such as steep slopes where you do not intend to walk. They will quickly smother the ground with a knee-high, weed-suppressing thicket of foliage. Apart from a once-a-year tidy up, they don't need any maintenance.

Flowering carpet Under trees and shrubs a flowering carpet of bulbs can be particularly effective. If you plant early varieties they will bloom before the overhead foliage emerges and then be hidden from view at other times. Choose shade-tolerant species that are suited to the impoverished conditions and mulch the soil well to conserve moisture and prevent weeds.

Gravel A popular option with many designers, gravel, pebbles and other aggregates are versatile and easy to lay. There are now many attractive grades and mixes to choose from including coloured glass chippings. If laid over a semi-permeable landscape fabric these surfaces are practically maintenance free. They are also easy to combine with plants to create a natural-looking effect.

Paving and decking These permanent ground coverings are maintenance-free, and there is a wide range of materials available to suit any garden design. Paving requires a lot of work before laying, particularly on a sloping site, and is an expensive option, requiring some skill. Decking is more versatile as it can be cut to fit any space and can be raised so that the ground does not have to be levelled beforehand. Decking requires basic do-it-yourself skills and costs about the same as paving.

PLANTING THROUGH GRAVEL

Draw back the gravel and make a cross-shaped slit in the base sheet. Plant normally, then firm in the plant, water well, and replace the flaps of the base sheet before re-covering with gravel.

Lawns are not the best option for every garden. In a small courtyard other coverings, such as gravel, might be a more sympathetic or appropriate material.

Patios

Paving requires careful thought and planning because, once laid, it is difficult and expensive to alter. First, consider what you want your paved area for and then identify the ideal position for a patio or paved area.

The purpose of the patio

A patio provides a smooth, level, hard surface on which to sit and relax and entertain. For these reasons patios are usually best sited in a spot that is not overlooked by neighbours and that is in a convenient position near to the house. If you want to use your patio for sunbathing it will need to catch the sun for much of the day, and if you want it for entertaining a site close to the kitchen would be most convenient.

In a north-facing garden, the best place to site a patio may be at the bottom of the garden to catch the maximum amount of sun. It may be more convenient to have two smaller areas of paving: one for sunbathing and one near to the house for entertaining. Wherever you decide to site your patio, make sure that the outlook is pleasing and that it is well screened; the privacy will create a relaxing atmosphere.

Deciding on a size

The size of the patio should also be determined by what you want to use it for. To accommodate a standard patio set of table and four chairs, you would need a paved area at least 3 x 3m (10 x 10ft) but preferably larger, about 4 x 4m (13 x 13ft), so that there is room to walk around the furniture comfortably while it is in use. However, in a small garden, the patio can dominate the garden and create an unbalanced effect in the overall design. In this situation you may be better off paving the whole garden and using planting

HOW TO LAY PAVING

1 Excavate the area to a depth that will allow for about 5cm (2in) of compacted hardcore topped with about 3–5cm (1–2in) of ballast, plus the thickness of the paving and mortar.

2 On top of the layers of hardcore and ballast, put five blobs of mortar where the slab is to be placed – one at each corner, and the other in the middle.

3 Position the slab carefully, bedding it down on the mortar. Over a large area of paving, create a slight slope to allow rainwater to run off freely.

4 Use a spirit (carpenter's) level placed over more than one slab to ensure that the slab is as close to horizontal as you want. Use a small wedge of wood under one end of the level to create a slight slope over the whole area if necessary. Tap the slab down further, or raise it by lifting and packing in more mortar.

5 Use spacers of an even thickness to ensure regular spacing between the paving slabs. Remove these later, before the joints are filled with mortar.

6 A day or two after laying the paving, go over it again to fill in the joints. Use a small pointing trowel and a dryish mortar mix. Finish off with a smooth stroke that leaves the mortar slightly recessed. This produces an attractive, crisp look. Brush any surplus mortar off the slabs before it dries.

pockets, raised beds and plenty of containers to provide visual interest in the garden.

Even in a large garden, expanses of paving can appear austere. You can break up this appearance by combining styles of paving as well as planting up the patio itself. Don't be tempted to overdo it because the effect will look too fussy and undermine the calm atmosphere.

Soften the boundary between the patio and lawn, perhaps with a low wall, designed with a planting cavity.

Check the depth of the foundation before you lay the paving. If it adjoins the house, make sure that the paving will end up at least 15cm (6in) below the damp-proof course.

Choosing materials

There is an incredibly wide range of materials suitable for garden paving. Which you choose is largely a matter of personal preference, although each type does have its own advantages and disadvantages. Try to choose a paving material that is sympathetic to the overall design and to the style of your house. Using materials that are already used elsewhere in the garden will help create a co-ordinated effect. Regularly shaped paving works well in a formal setting, whereas paving that consists of smaller units or a range of paving sizes is often a better choice if you are trying to create a more relaxed feel. If you are combining different materials, make sure they are the same thickness to make laying easier.

RIGHT
The top row shows (from left to right) natural stone sett, clay paver, brick, artificial sett.

The centre row shows a range of the different shapes of concrete paving blocks available.

The bottom row shows some of the colours and sizes of concrete paving slabs available.

Grouping containers together presents an attractive display to brighten up the patio. Here, *Clematis* 'Prince Charles' is planted in a chimney pot next to some potted chives.

Decking

Garden decking is a popular choice these days and in many situations is often the best option. It can be cheaper and easier to construct than paving, especially on a sloping site, and provides a hard, flat surface that is functional and looks good too.

Designing with decking

Decking can be tailor-made to suit any garden design. Its essentially natural appearance makes it ideal for informal gardens where you can make the most of the warm tones of the timber. Decking also looks good in a bold, contemporary garden design. Indeed, it can be made the main focal point by choosing an eye-catching design and colouring it with woodstain. In a formal setting, emphasize the clean lines of a deck by using stepped edges.

Different designs can be achieved by fixing planks in different ways (see opposite), but on the whole, it is best to keep any pattern fairly simple. In some countries there are building codes that may have to be met. If in doubt, seek professional help with the design, even if you intend to construct it yourself.

Timber decking provides a durable, practical and easy-to-care-for floor surface. It makes a refreshing change from a patio made of paving slabs or bricks. Adding containers will help to make the deck a pleasant place to sit in summer.

HOW TO MAKE A DECK

1 Level the area, then use bricks or building blocks to support your decking. Calculate the position of each row. Each timber bearer should be supported in the middle as well as the ends. Excavate the soil and position the brick.

2 Position each block so that about half of it sits in the soil – it is important that air circulates beneath the bearers. Tap down each block to ensure it is level, adding or removing soil if necessary.

3 Use a spirit (carpenter's) level to ensure that the blocks are level. If the ground is unstable, set the bricks or blocks on pads of concrete. Make sure that they are level, or the final decking will not be stable.

Which timber?

Decking can be made from hardwood, pressure-treated softwood or plain softwood. Hardwood decks made from white oak or western red cedar are durable and practically maintenance free, but they cost a lot more to construct. Decking made from pressure-treated (tanalized) softwood is less expensive and reasonably durable, but requires seasonal maintenance, while plain softwood decking needs regular maintenance and is prone to rotting, so it is not very durable. Clad the deck with non-slip grooved planks spaced about 6mm (¼in) apart to allow for expansion and to allow water to drain away freely. Attach them with galvanized nails or screws. All decks should also be laid on a sheet of semi-permeable material such as landscaping fabric.

Choosing a deck

The easiest way to create a deck is to use ready-made decking tiles that can be laid straight on to a firm, flat surface, such an old patio, roof terrace or firmed hardcore. For a better result, lay the tiles on top of a framework of pressure-treated timber and treat any cut ends or joints with wood preservative. You can also get decks in kit form, and these are very easy to put together and a good choice where the deck isn't fitted into a particular space, such as an island deck part-way down the garden.

Custom-made decking, supplied and fitted by a professional supplier, is the most convenient but most expensive option. Specialist suppliers will take on the whole process, from planning, checking local planning regulations and getting the permissions necessary to constructing the deck. With custom-made decking you can be more ambitious with split levels, walkways and even raised decks to give the perfect view of the garden.

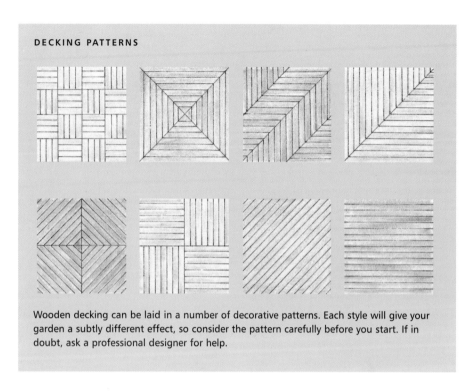

DECKING PATTERNS

Wooden decking can be laid in a number of decorative patterns. Each style will give your garden a subtly different effect, so consider the pattern carefully before you start. If in doubt, ask a professional designer for help.

4 Use wood preservative on the bearers if necessary. Space out the bearers on the block supports. Add extra bearers near the ends and sides of the decking, where planks (boards) will need extra support.

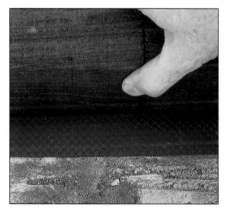

5 Your bearers may not be long enough to stretch the whole length of the deck, in which case make sure joints are made above a block. Use a damp-proofing strip between each block and bearer to prevent water seeping up.

6 Add a plastic sheet to suppress weeds, then saw the decking planks to size and treat with a preservative. Nail in position with galvanized nails leaving gaps of about 6mm (¼in) between planks to allow for expansion.

Beds and borders

The position, size and shape of beds and borders should be considered at the outset of a new garden design, as they have an enormous influence on the way the garden is viewed.

Changing the perspective

Most gardeners consider beds and borders essential, both to grow specific plants and to add interest to the shape of the garden. It is quite easy to change the shape of a border, so consider whether the existing design is making the most effective use of perspective. For example, narrow borders that simply follow the boundary lines will make a narrow garden seem narrower and a short garden shorter.

Create the illusion of space in a small garden by disguising the boundary. Wider borders provide the opportunity to combine a range of plants that together will either hide the boundary from view or break up its outline, effectively camouflaging it. Dividing the garden horizontally will also make the garden more intriguing because at least part of the design is hidden from view, encouraging the casual visitor to explore. In a short garden, use a long, curving border cutting across the garden to make it seem longer, emphasizing the longest dimension, the diagonal.

Breaking up a lawn

A large area of grass can make a garden look plain, and you may want to add a feature such as an island bed or a border alongside a path.

HOW TO CREATE A CIRCULAR BED

1 Insert a post in the centre of the proposed bed. Attach one end of a piece of string to the post and the other end to a bottle filled with sand or soil.

2 Walk slowly around the post, keeping the string taut and the bottle tilted, so that the sand or soil trickles out and marks the outline of the circle.

3 Once the circle is complete, the turf can be cut from within the marked area in order to produce a perfectly circular bed.

HOW TO CREATE AN OVAL BED

Place two posts in the ground and loosely tie a piece of string around them. Experiment with the distance between the posts and the length of the piece of string to get the size and shape of bed you require. Place a bottle filled with sand or soil inside the loop of string and walk around the posts, keeping the string taut. The sand or soil will trickle out, creating the outline of a perfect oval.

HOW TO CREATE AN IRREGULAR BED

Use a flexible garden hose to work out the size and shape of an irregular bed. Once you are happy with the shape of the bed, remove a line of turf around the inside edge of the hose to mark it out.

This will break up the garden visually, and also give you the chance to grow more flowers and shrubs. It can sometimes be more effective to cut a bed towards one end of the lawn rather than in a central position. This can make the most of your lawn by taking the eye across it to the flower bed.

It is important to keep an island bed looking neat as it is a key focal point. However, by choosing low-maintenance plants such as alpines, and mulching with an attractive layer of gravel, an island bed doesn't need to be time-consuming.

Choosing plants

It is essential to choose the right combination of plants for each part of the site. First, consider what you want the plants to do. If you want year-round cover you will need a high proportion of evergreens to provide the screen. But a garden made from evergreens alone becomes very static and lacking in interest. In this situation, make the key plants that block the sight lines evergreen, but fill in and around them with a range of deciduous plants, bulbs and herbaceous plants to add seasonal variety and excitement.

Beds of lavender flank a narrow path. It's a good choice of plant: brushing past the lavender will release its delicious scent.

HOW TO PREPARE THE GROUND

1 Since flowerbeds and borders are likely to be undisturbed for many years it is important to clear the area of weeds first. There are three ways of doing this: spray with weedkiller, skim off the surface with a hoe, or cover with polythene for several months.

2 Dig the first trench to one spade's depth across the plot, and transfer the soil you have removed to the other end of the plot using a barrow where it will be used to fill in the final trench.

3 Fork a layer of well-rotted compost or manure into the bottom of the trench to improve the soil structure and to provide nutrients for the plants.

4 Dig the next trench across the plot, turning the soil on to the compost in the first trench. Add compost to the new trench and then dig the next.

5 Continue down the border until the whole of the surface has been turned. Add some compost to the final trench and then fill with the soil taken from the first.

6 If possible, dig in the autumn and allow the winter weather to break down the soil. In spring, take out any new weeds and rake over the bed.

Raised beds

Although they are time consuming and expensive to build, raised beds can solve a range of gardening problems, such as poor soil or bad drainage, but they are also useful for adding interest to flat plots or for providing level ground in sloping gardens.

Designing with raised beds

Raised beds offer so many advantages that it is surprising they do not feature in more gardens. They are ideal for adding height and interest to otherwise boringly flat gardens, but equally they are a practical solution to providing level areas on sloping ground. In small gardens they can be combined with paving to produce an intimate courtyard garden. Raised beds can be a functional square or rectangle, or designed to fit a corner in the garden.

Choosing the right soil

Raised beds hold a lot more soil than containers, so they are much easier to look after and you can grow much bigger plants. They also offer the opportunity to grow plants in your garden that otherwise would fail to thrive. For example, if your soil is poor or badly drained, raised beds can be filled with good quality imported loam. Indeed, if you fancy growing plants that like a specific

HOW TO MAKE A RAISED BED USING BRICKS

1 Mark out the shape of the bed using short pointed stakes and string. Use a builders' set square (triangle) to ensure the correct angles. Define the lines with a thin stream of fine sand or use line-marker paint.

2 Dig out along the markings to a depth of 30cm (12in) and width of 15cm (6in). Fill with concrete to within 5cm (2in) of the top. Firm down, level and leave for 24 hours to set. For concrete, use 1 part cement to 4 parts ballast.

3 Build up four or five courses of bricks and set each into mortar, checking with a spirit (carpenter's) level at every stage.

4 Clean up the mortar while it is still wet with a pointing trowel. Leave it to harden.

5 Before filling with soil, coat the inside of the wall with a waterproof paint.

6 Put in a layer of rubble topped with gravel for drainage. Fill with topsoil and stir in a layer of a good potting medium.

7 Plant up the raised bed in the usual manner and water in well.

8 The completed bed planted with a selection of culinary herbs and wild strawberries.

type of soil, such as acid-loving rhododendrons, raised beds filled with ericaceous compost (soil mix) will provide that opportunity even if your garden soil is not suitable.

The soil in raised beds warms up more quickly than garden soil so you can start off new plants earlier in spring, which is useful if you grow early vegetables or flowers. For anyone who finds bending difficult, raised beds are particularly welcome.

Which material?

Traditional permanent raised beds made from bricks or blocks are built in much the same way as solid brick retaining walls, the only differences being that the walls in a raised bed are built vertical rather than slightly sloping. They can made from bricks or blocks mortared together, with "weep-holes" (vertical joints free of mortar) every metre (yard) or so along the base of each wall to allow water to drain out. Check the bricks are frostproof; ordinary housebricks may not be suitable. In a cottage-style garden, dry-stone walls also make good raised beds, with cracks and crevices used to grow plants.

Raised beds can also be constructed from wood. Old railway sleepers (railroad ties) were traditionally recommended, but designer mini-sleepers are more readily available from garden centres, either as individual logs that can be nailed together tailored to suit any position, or as part of a raised bed kit, which is easily slotted together. Pressure-treated softwood gravel boards, which will withstand damp, are an economical material for making simple raised beds for the vegetable garden. Alternatively, once the boards have been stained they will make an attractive feature container on the patio.

Growing a mix of fragrant herbs in a raised bed will bring the scents, colours and textures closer to you, making a feature of this attractive part of the garden.

HOW TO MAKE A RAISED BED USING WOOD

1 Set the log edging in position and tap it into place. Check with a spirit (carpenter's) level. If you are using flexible edging, drive in stakes to which you nail the edging.

2 On geometric shapes, as shown here, nail the corners together with rust-proof nails.

3 Fill with soil, ensuring that you create the correct conditions for the types of plant you are intending to grow. Heathers will need an acid soil to grow well.

4 Plant up the raised bed and water the plants in well. Mulch the ground with shredded bark or gravel to retain moisture.

Paths

Paths exert a strong influence on the design and sense of movement in a garden, so consider the effect during the planning process. It is also essential to match the construction to the type of use a path will receive.

Designing with paths

A path's design should reflect the overall theme of the garden. In a formal setting straight paths with clean lines will reinforce the formality of the design, whereas in an informal garden gently meandering paths will be more appropriate. Try to avoid straight paths that lead the eye directly to the bottom of the garden, because they will be less inviting and make the plot seem smaller. Calm the feeling of movement by adding changes in direction along the path and create a sense of mystery by allowing the path to disappear from view – behind a garden structure or border, for example.

Temporary paths

Roll-up plastic paths are useful for protecting areas of the garden when heavy one-off construction projects or seasonal heavy maintenance tasks are being carried out. They are particularly useful for protecting lawns during the autumn and winter months. Builders' planks (boards) are another option.

Which path?

There are three main types of path: functional paths that are constantly used come rain or come shine; occasional paths that are largely ornamental and are used infrequently or not at all; and temporary paths that are rolled out for specific jobs. All paths should have a slight slope or camber to prevent puddles forming in wet weather.

Regularly used paths

A well-used path needs to be at least 60cm (2ft) wide and have an all-weather surface. If laid against the side of the house the path needs to be at least 15cm (6in) below the

HOW TO LAY A GRAVEL PATH

1 Excavate the area to a depth of about 15cm (6in), and ram the base firm.

2 Provide a stout edge to retain the gravel. For a straight path, securing battens by pegs about 1m (3ft) apart is an easy and inexpensive method.

3 Place a layer of compacted hardcore. Add a mixture of sand and coarse gravel (you can use sand and gravel mixture sold as ballast). Rake level and tamp or roll until firm.

4 Top up to within 2.5cm (1in) of the edge or battens with the final grade of gravel. In small gardens the size often known as pea gravel looks good and is easy to walk on. Rake the gravel level.

A winding gravel path, bordered with carefully chosen cottage garden plants, is an inviting way to the front door.

damp-proof course and slope gently away from the house to shed water.

The amount and type of traffic a path will carry is one of the main considerations when you decide the type of path to opt for. Paved paths, using concrete slabs set on blobs of mortar on a solid base of rammed hardcore, are the best choice for an all-weather path that's used for regular foot and light wheeled traffic (bikes, wheelbarrows etc). This type of path is expensive, a lot of work to construct and not very adaptable.

Paved paths made from small unit paving blocks bedded into a layer of sharp sand on top of well-firmed soil are less expensive and are easier to construct. They can be adapted to any design, but you do need to have solid edges to the path to keep the paving in place. These can be wooden, concrete or simply a row of blocks set in a foundation of concrete.

Gravel paths are simple to construct on firmed soil with an underlay of membrane. They can be made any shape, including complicated curves. Little maintenance is required apart from removing the odd weed and the occasional rake to keep it looking neat. Unfortunately, the gravel tends to be kicked into nearby borders and may get walked into the house.

Occasionally used paths

Paths constructed for largely ornamental reasons can be made from a wider range of materials. In general, choose a material that is in keeping with its surroundings and will provide a solid footing. Stepping stones made from the paving used elsewhere in the garden can look good set into the lawn to provide access to the washing line. Under trees or through a shrubbery, log stepping stones or a path of chipped bark can be more appropriate.

Neat edging

For a period garden, Victorian-style rope edging looks appropriate. You can use it either to retain a gravel path or as an edging to a paved path.

Wavy edgings such as this are also reminiscent of some of the older styles of garden, but they can also be used in a modern setting to create a formal effect.

HOW TO LAY BRICKS AND BLOCKS

1 Excavate the area and prepare a sub-base of about 5cm (2in) of compacted hardcore or sand-and-gravel mix. Set an edging along one end and side first. Check that it is level, then lay the pavers on a bed of mortar.

2 Once the edging is set, lay a 5cm (2in) bed of sharp sand over the area. Use a straight-edged piece of wood to level the surface. Position the pavers, butting them tightly to the edging and to each other.

3 Brush loose sand into the joints of the pavers with a broom. Hire a flat-plate vibrator to consolidate the sand or tamp the pavers down with a club hammer used over a piece of wood.

4 Brush in more sand and repeat the vibrating process once more for a firm, neat finish. To avoid damage do not go too close to an unsupported edge with the vibrator. The path should be ready to use straight away.

Walls

Although walls are mainly thought of as a structure to provide security and privacy along the boundary, they are also useful within a garden for building terracing on a sloping plot as well as a range of other features, including raised beds, barbecues, garden screens, seats and plinths for containers and ornaments.

Most builders' merchants have a wide range of bricks suitable for garden walls. Bricks come in many colours and finishes and these are just a small selection of the many available.

Designing with walls

Walls can be made from a wide range of materials so can be constructed to suit any style. Substantial or prominent walls, such as those used along the boundary, will fit in more easily with the rest of the garden if they are constructed of the same material used for the house. Smaller walls within the garden can be designed to reflect the overall design of the garden. They can also be combined with other materials, such as wooden trellis, to help soften the overall effect.

Which wall?

There are basically four types of wall: free-standing walls for boundaries and screens; solid retaining walls for terracing; loose dry-stone walls also for terracing; and retaining walls for raised beds. All walls require some skill to construct, so if you are in doubt seek professional advice.

Plants for wall crevices

Aubrieta deltoidea
Campanula portenschlagiana
Dianthus deltoides
Erinus alpinus
Erodium reichardii
Geranium sanguineum var. *striatum*
Mentha requienii
Pratia pedunculata
Saxifraga paniculata
Scabiosa graminifolia
Sedum spathulifolium

Foundations

All walls need a concrete foundation along their entire length. The higher the wall, the wider and deeper the foundations have to be. For walls up to 75cm (30in) high the foundations should be 10cm (4in) deep and about twice as wide as the wall being constructed. For walls over 75cm (30in) high, foundations should be 15cm (6in) deep and about three times as wide as the wall.

Boundary walls

The way a boundary wall is constructed will also depend on how high you want to build it. A small wall at the front of the house could be made from single bricks, 10cm (4in) thick, if it is up to 45cm (18in). Any higher, and you will either have to use a double brick wall, 23cm (9in) thick, or build supporting piers every couple of metres (yards) along a single brick wall. Walls over 1.2m (4ft) need a double-brick construction and supporting piers. Add coping stones on top of the wall to help shed water and to protect the bricks.

BRICK BONDING

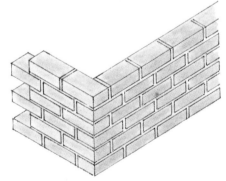

Running bond or stretcher bond The simplest form of bonding used for walls a single brick wide.

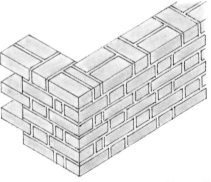

Flemish bond Creates a strong bond in a wall two bricks wide. Bricks are laid lengthways and across the wall in the same course.

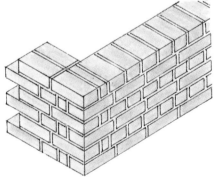

English bond Used for a thick wall where strength is needed. Alternate courses are laid lengthways then across the wall.

Retaining walls

Solid retaining walls are made from bricks or blocks mortared together. The wall will have to be strong enough to hold back the weight of the soil behind it. For this reason, always use the double-brick construction method but this time lay the foundations and build the wall so that it slopes back slightly. Leave weep-holes (vertical joints free of mortar) every metre (yard) or so along the base of the wall to allow water to drain out from the soil. Pack in rubble behind the weep-holes and cover with coarse gravel to

prevent soil washing out and to stop the weep-holes from becoming blocked with soil.

Dry-stone walls also make good retaining walls up to 1m (3ft) high. Again the wall needs to be built so that it leans back slightly. The blocks should be selected so that they interlock as much as possible, leaving few gaps. Pack rubble behind the wall as you go to help secure each layer in place. Any large crevices can be planted with suitable plants.

Retaining walls provide an excellent opportunity to experiment with climbers and wall shrubs.

A wall is cloaked in the scented creamy white flowers of *Rosa* 'Climbing Iceberg'.

HOW TO BUILD A WALL

1 All walls require a footing. For a low wall this is one brick wide; for larger and thicker walls the dimensions are increased. Excavate a trench about 30cm (12in) deep and put 13cm (5in) of consolidated hardcore in the bottom. Drive pegs in so that the tops are at the final height of the foundation. Use a spirit (carpenter's) level to check that they are level.

2 To form the foundations, fill the trench with a concrete mix of 2 parts cement, 5 parts sharp sand and 7 parts 2cm (¾in) aggregate, and level it off with the top of the pegs. Use a straight-edged board to tamp the concrete down and remove any air pockets.

3 When the concrete foundation has hardened for a few days, lay the bricks on a bed of mortar, adding a wedge of mortar at one end of each brick as you lay them. For a single brick wall with supporting piers, the piers should be positioned at each end and at 1.8–2.4m (6–8ft) intervals, and can be made by laying two bricks crossways.

4 For subsequent courses, lay a ribbon of mortar on top of the previous row, then "butter" one end of the brick to be laid.

5 Tap level, checking constantly with a spirit (carpenter's) level to make sure that the wall is level and vertical.

6 The top of the wall is best finished off with a coping of suitable bricks or with special coping stones sold for the purpose.

Fences

One of the most popular choices for marking a boundary, fences offer instant privacy and security. They are less expensive to construct than a wall and need less maintenance than a hedge.

Designing with fences

There is a huge selection of fencing styles in a range of different materials, including various woods, metals and plastic, so you should have no problem finding a style that will enhance your garden. In the front garden fences with a more open structure are often used. Examples include picket or post-and-rail fences, ranch-style fences and post-and-chain fences. They do not provide privacy or much security, but they are an attractive way of marking the boundary.

In most back gardens, a boundary fence should recede from view, so choose something robust enough to support climbers and wall shrubs that will help disguise it. However, in certain circumstances you might want to make a feature of a fence. Painting with a woodstain used

A fence has been erected to screen the practical corner of the garden from view. It is strong enough to support a climber.

elsewhere in the garden or to co-ordinate with a nearby planting scheme will emphasize its presence.

Which fence?

The most popular type of fence is the ready-made panel, which comes in various forms, including horizontal

lap, vertical lap and interwoven. They are also available in several heights including 1.2m (4ft), 1.5m (5ft) and 1.8m (6ft). Fencing panels are very cheap and easy to put up between regularly spaced, well-anchored posts. Most fencing panels are rather flimsy and have a lifespan of less

HOW TO ERECT A RANCH-STYLE FENCE

1 The posts of a ranch-style fence must be well secured in the ground. Use 10cm (4in) square posts, set at 2m (6½ft) intervals. For additional strength add 8cm (3in) square intermediate posts. Make sure the posts go at least 45cm (18in) into the ground. Concrete the posts into position, then fill in with soil.

2 Screw or nail the planks (boards) in place, making sure that the fixings are galvanized. Use a spirit (carpenter's) level to check that the planks are horizontal. Butt-join the planks in the centre of a post but try to stagger the joints on each row so that there is not a weak point in the fence.

3 Fit a post cap to improve the appearance and also protect the posts. Paint with a good quality paint recommended for outdoor use. Choose the colour of the paint carefully; you will need to keep white paint clean in order for the fence to look good.

than ten years, even when regularly maintained. For a better quality and longer-lasting wooden fence, opt for the close-board fencing. Here, a structure of posts with two or three cross-members, called arris rails, is constructed before cladding with wooden strips. These are sometimes thinner along one edge than the other and are overlapped when nailed to the arris rails. Alternatively the fence can be regular, where the pales are nailed on to the arris rails butted together with no spaces between them and without overlapping.

Posts

With all types of fence, the posts should be durable. For preference choose a naturally rot-resistant hardwood, but pressure-treated softwood is more commonly available. With panel fencing they are set 1.8m (6ft) apart to accommodate the panel, but with close-board fencing they are usually spaced more widely – 2.4–3m (8–10ft). Either buy posts that are long enough for the bottom section to be buried into the ground and held firm with concrete, or buy posts the same height as the fence and secure them with special fencing spikes.

Planning permission

Check with your local planning authority before erecting a new wall or fence to make sure there are no restrictions. In certain circumstances, particularly in front gardens near to a highway or in designated conservation areas, there may be restrictions on the type and height of boundary you are allowed to erect. Normally, you require planning consent for any wall more than 1.8m (6ft) high and for a wall more than 1m (3ft) high that abuts a highway.

HOW TO ERECT A PANEL FENCE

1 Post spikes are an easier option than excavating holes and concreting the post in position. Use a special tool to protect the spike top, then drive it in with a sledge-hammer. Check with a spirit (carpenter's) level to ensure it is absolutely vertical.

2 Insert the post in the spike, checking the vertical again, then lay the panel in position on the ground and mark the position of the next post. Drive in the next spike, testing for the vertical again.

3 There are various ways to fix the panels to the posts, but panel brackets are easy to use. Simply nail the brackets to the posts.

4 Lift the panel and nail in position, through the brackets. Insert the post at the other end and nail the panel in position at that end.

5 Check the horizontal level both before and after nailing, and make any necessary adjustments before moving on to the next panel.

6 Finish off by nailing a post cap to the top of each post. This will keep water out of the end grain of the timber and extend its life.

Other garden structures

Pergolas, trellises and arches are not only quick and easy to construct but, if correctly positioned, can also effectively transform the appearance of a garden. Flatpack kits are now available in a variety of materials and styles to suit both traditional and contemporary gardens.

Designing with arches, trellises and pergolas

Arches can perform several functions in the garden. They look lovely when positioned over a path and festooned with colourful climbing plants. Ideally, the structure should frame a distant object, such as an ornament, or focus the eye on the path as it leads tantalizingly out of sight into the next area of the garden. Arches can also be used to link borders either side of the garden to give the overall design coherence.

Trellises can be used to divide the garden into separate "rooms" and add a strong vertical dimension to an otherwise flat garden scheme. If you are looking for a more subtle application, a trellis can provide a secluded corner for a garden seat, creating a peaceful sitting area or arbour.

A pergola is simply an open structure, often placed over a patio adjacent to the house to create an intimate area for outdoor entertaining. It can be covered in shading materials, such as netting or bamboo screens, or a more natural covering of climbers. Pergolas also can be used away from the house, forming a covered walkway along the sunny side of the garden or a point of focus in the middle of the garden. Being a larger structure means that a pergola lends itself to supporting quite vigorous climbers, such as wisteria, which would swamp an arch or trellis.

Adding a fence or trellis will not only give your garden a strong sense of design, but it also provides a wonderful opportunity to grow climbers.

Choosing materials

In an informal or country-style garden, structures made from rustic poles blend naturally into their surroundings. These can be bought as ready-made structures from fencing suppliers or made from fresh-cut wood. Rustic poles are usually roughly jointed and nailed together with galvanized nails. Rustic structures are not usually as strong as other types and often require more cross-members to improve their rigidity and strength.

If you are using sawn timber for arches and pergolas, choose timber that has been pressure-treated with preservative to prevent it rotting.

HOW TO ASSEMBLE AN ARCH

1 The simplest way to make an arch is to use a kit, which only needs assembling. First, establish the post positions, allowing a gap between the edge of the path and post, so that plants do not obstruct the path.

2 Dig four 60cm (2ft) deep holes to hold the posts. Alternatively, choose a kit with shorter posts for use with fence spikes. Drive the spikes in with a special tool, using a spirit (carpenter's) level to ensure they are vertical.

Scented climbers for garden structures

Akebia quinata
Clematis armandii
Clematis montana
Clematis rehderiana
Jasminum officinale and 'Fiona Sunrise'
Lonicera x *americana*
Lonicera japonica 'Halliana'
Lonicera periclymenum 'Belgica'
    and 'Serotina'
Rosa 'Bobbie James', 'Gloire de Dijon',
    'Madame Alfred Carrière', 'New
    Dawn' and 'Zéphirine Drouhin'
Trachelospermum jasminoides
    and 'Variegatum'
Wisteria sinensis

There are two main styles of wooden pergola: traditional and oriental. The traditional style has fewer, larger roofing timbers with square-cut ends, while oriental-style pergolas have bevelled ends.

You can also get plastic-coated tubular metal arches, arbours and pergolas. These are lightweight and so easier to put up than wooden versions. Their stylish appearance makes them suitable for use in contemporary garden designs.

HOW TO JOIN RUSTIC POLES

If you need to attach a horizontal pole to a vertical one, saw a notch of a suitable size in the top of the vertical one so that the horizontal piece will fit snugly on top.

To join two horizontal pieces of wood, saw two opposing and matching notches so that one sits over the other. Secure the two pieces with galvanized nails or screws.

To fix cross-pieces to horizontals or uprights, remove a V-shaped notch, using a chisel if necessary to achieve a snug fit, then nail into place with galvanized nails.

Use halving joints where two poles cross. Make two saw cuts halfway through the pole, then remove the waste timber with a chisel. Secure the two pieces with galvanized nails or screws.

Bird's mouth joints are useful for connecting horizontal or diagonal pieces to uprights. Cut out a V-shaped notch about 3cm (1in) deep and saw the other piece of timber to match the shape. You may need to use a chisel to achieve a good fit.

Try out the assembly on the ground, then insert the uprights in prepared holes and make sure these are secure before adding any further pieces. Most pieces can be nailed together, but screw any sections subject to stress. Use rust-free screws and nails.

3 Position the legs of the arch in the holes. Backfill with the excavated earth and compact with your heel. Check that the legs are vertical using a spirit level. If using spikes, insert the legs and then tighten any securing bolts.

4 The next stage is to construct the overhead beams of the arch. Lay both halves on a large flat surface and carefully screw the joint together at the correct angle. Use galvanized screws to protect the arch from corrosion.

5 Fit the overhead beams to the posts. In this example they slot into the tops of the posts and are nailed in place.

Preparing the soil

Cultivation is the basis of all good soil husbandry and is the starting point of most gardening activity. Even a garden run on a no-dig system requires thorough cultivation to get it off to a good start.

Digging is the best way of removing weeds and other unwanted debris from the soil, breaking up compacted layers and incorporating organic matter. It also brings pests to the surface so that they can be eaten by birds and introduces air into the soil. However, once planted and mulched with a thick layer of organic matter there may be no need to dig it again provided the soil is not walked on, which will compact it.

Well-rotted garden compost is one of the best soil conditioners. Every garden should have a compost heap, where grass clippings, leaves and other vegetable matter can be left to rot down. Not only is this material absolutely free, but it is an environmentally sound practice.

Look after your soil and it will look after you – requiring less effort and providing reliable bumper harvests.

Know your soil

It is essential that you understand what type of soil you have in your garden and its level of fertility before you can take steps to improve it. Several simple soil-testing kits are available to help you.

Understanding your soil

All soils are made up of the same basic ingredients: clay, silt and sand. It is the proportions of these that determines the type of soil you have.

Clay soil This heavy soil is generally fertile, but is sticky and difficult to work. The tiny clay particles pack together tightly with few air spaces between them, so the soil cannot drain freely and remains wet for longer. This causes problems in spring, because the soil is too wet to be cultivated and remains colder for longer. Soils with a high clay content have a poor structure and compact easily when walked on, further impeding drainage. When clay soils dry out in summer they crack badly and form solid lumps.

Sandy soil The particles in sandy soil are mainly larger and irregularly shaped, which means that water

It is essential that you choose plants that like the prevailing soil conditions in your garden. The rock rose (*Helianthemum*), for example, will thrive in neutral to alkaline soil in a dry, sunny spot.

drains freely and there are plenty of air spaces between the particles. The downside of free-draining, sandy soils is that nutrients are very easily leached (washed) out, which leaves the soil impoverished. Free-draining soils are also more prone to drought during dry spells. However, they are quicker to warm up after winter and easy to work, so are ideal for sowing early crops in spring.

Silt soil In terms of particle size, silt falls roughly between clay and sand. The soil is usually fertile. Silty soils are reasonably free-draining, but like clay soils they are easily compacted.

Loamy soil This type of soil contains both clay and sand particles as well as silt, and in many ways they offer the best of all worlds, being highly fertile and reasonably well drained, but still fairly moisture-

HOW TO TEST THE SOIL FOR NUTRIENTS

1 Collect a soil sample from 10cm (4in) below the surface. Take a number of samples, and mix together for a representative test.

2 Follow the instructions on the kit. Mix one part of soil with five parts of water. Shake well in a jar, then allow the water to settle.

3 Draw off some of the settled liquid from the top few centimetres (about an inch) for your test.

retentive. Loamy soils also warm up quickly in spring so are suitable for growing early crops.

The other essential factor about your soil that will affect the plants you can grow is its acidity or alkalinity. This is measured on a pH scale, of which the mid-point, 7, is neutral. Anything higher than that is increasingly alkaline, anything lower is increasingly acidic. Most plants prefer a neutral to slightly acidic soil (down to pH 5.5), although they will tolerate slightly alkaline conditions (up to pH 7.5). A few plants, such as azaleas, need acidic conditions to thrive; others, such as lilacs, prefer slightly alkaline soils.

Assessing your soil

If you have a new garden or are planting a new area, it is worth finding out what your soil is like so that you can improve it before planting. The first step is to check the drainage by digging holes about 30cm (12in) deep randomly across the area. Fill each with water and see how quickly it drains. If it all disappears within 24 hours all is

Reducing soil acidity

The acidity of your soil can be reduced by adding lime some weeks before planting and working it in thoroughly with a rake. First, check the soil with a soil-testing kit to see how much lime is required.

well. If the hole is still partly full after that time, you may have a drainage problem. In most cases this can be overcome by digging deeply and incorporating plenty of well-rotted organic matter and grit into the soil. Otherwise, you will have to get land drains installed or build raised beds.

Testing your soil

Cheap and reliable soil-testing kits are available from garden retailers that will indicate the nutrient balance in your soil and its pH level. For this to be of value you must test a representative sample of soil. The most reliable way of doing this is to lay four canes on the soil surface in a large W shape, then use a trowel to

Soil-testing kits of various degrees of sophistication are widely available, such as this electronic meter to test the pH level.

dig a small hole, about 15cm (6in) deep, at each point of the W, making a total of five holes. Scoop out some soil from each hole and place it in a garden sieve over a bucket. This will remove any debris and large pieces of organic matter. Mix the soil from the different holes thoroughly before testing. Make sure you do not test contaminated areas, such as where a compost heap has been, otherwise the results will not be representative of the garden as a whole.

4 Use a pipette to transfer the solution to the test chamber in the plastic container supplied with the kit.

5 Select a colour-coded capsule (one for each nutrient). Put the powder in the chamber, replace the cap and shake well.

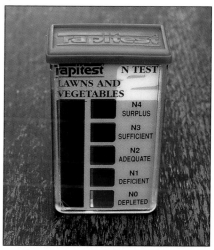

6 After a few minutes, compare the colour of the liquid with the shade panel shown on the container.

Improving your soil

With the knowledge of what your soil is like, you can take positive steps to improve it through the incorporation of well-rotted manure and compost and thorough digging.

Soil conditioning

Organic matter, such as well-rotted farmyard manure, garden compost or mushroom compost, will improve all but peaty soils, which are already rich in the material. It improves the structure of heavy soils by allowing water and air in, and helps sandy soils by acting as a sponge, holding on to moisture. It also provides food for beneficial soil-borne creatures, such as earthworms, which further aerate the soil.

When well-rotted, organic matter is practically odourless it is ready to add to the soil. Do not use fresh or partly rotted organic material because the micro-organisms will use nitrogen to complete the process and this will be extracted from your soil.

Heavy soils are best dug in late autumn, to allow the large clods to be broken down by frost action. Loamy soils can be dug at any time in winter, as long as the soil conditions allow. Light, sandy soils are best cultivated in spring to avoid loss of nutrients through leaching in winter.

Forking

Light, recently cultivated soils can be simply forked over to the full depth of a garden fork, incorporating organic matter as you work. The soil is roughly turned and placed back in the same position. Remove any weeds and other debris by hand.

Digging

There are three main methods used to dig the garden, simple, single and double digging, although there are variations of each.

HOW TO CARRY OUT DOUBLE DIGGING

1 Dig a wide trench, placing the topsoil on a plastic sheet to one side to be used later when filling in the final trench.

2 Break up the subsoil at the bottom of the trench, adding well-rotted manure to the soil as you proceed.

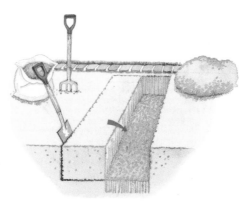

3 Dig the next trench, turning the topsoil over on top of the broken subsoil that is in the first trench.

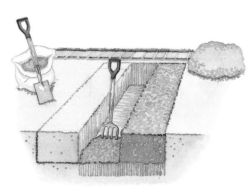

4 Continue down the plot, taking care that subsoil from the lower trench is not mixed with topsoil from the upper.

Simple digging As its name suggests this is the least complicated to do. It is useful for cultivating lighter soils and for removing weeds. The spade is forced vertically into the soil to the full depth of the blade and the handle is eased back to lever the earth up. The spade is turned and the soil deposited in the same place but inverted, burying annual weeds at the bottom of the excavation. Perennial weeds and other debris are removed by hand, and clods of soil are broken up with sharp jabs of the spade. Repeat the technique across the plot. When the other side is reached, step back about 15cm (6in) and repeat the procedure across the plot.

Preparing for planting

You should prepare the soil for planting in the spring, when the surface of the soil is dry. Simply rake level using a soil rake, removing any stones that have made their way to the surface as well as any weed seedlings. Any remaining clods should break down readily to form a breadcrumb-like structure (known as a fine tilth), which is ideal for sowing and planting. If necessary, suitable fertilizers can be added at this point.

Avoid walking on the soil at any time because your weight will cause compaction. Instead, always lay short planks on the surface to spread your weight and work from these.

Single digging Used on heavier soils, this is a very good technique for incorporating organic matter into the upper layer of soil. It follows the same process as simple digging, except a trench about 30cm (12in) wide is excavated across the plot and the soil deposited on one side. A layer of well-rotted garden compost or manure is placed in the bottom of the trench. Moving 15cm (6in) back, the next row is dug, but the excavated soil is thrown forward to fill the first trench. After two passes across the plot the first trench will have been filled and a second trench created. This process is repeated until the entire plot has been dug. The excavated soil from the first trench is moved to the other end of the plot to fill the last trench.

Double digging This goes one step further and is used to break up compacted subsoil or for preparing deep beds for hungry crops. After excavating each trench, use a garden fork to loosen the subsoil at the bottom of the trench and mix in well-rotted organic matter or grit to improve the drainage if required. Then follow the procedure for single digging. It is important not to mix the soils from each layer.

This border was prepared thoroughly before planting. The soil was dug over to remove weeds and stones and to improve the soil structure. Plenty of organic compost was added to improve drainage. The end result is a border full of strong, healthy plants that requires little maintenance.

Using a cultivator

It is worth considering mechanical digging if you have a large plot to cultivate. However, you will need to clear the perennial weeds beforehand, and cultivators are hard work and noisy to operate. If a mechanical digger is used repeatedly on the same plot, the soil structure will suffer and a compacted layer can form just below the maximum depth of penetration of the blades.

HOW TO PREPARE FOR PLANTING

1 Break down the soil into a fine crumbly structure, and level with a rake before sowing.

2 Any large clods that still exist should be broken down with a spade or fork or the back of a rake. Try to avoid walking on the soil as this will cause compaction.

3 Once the soil is reasonably fine, rake it level. At the same time remove any large stones and other debris.

Making compost and leafmould

Composting is good for your garden and good for the environment. It is a convenient way of getting rid of garden waste and will also save you money, so it is well worth making the effort to do it.

Garden compost

Making your own compost is sound sense. It returns organic matter and nutrients to the soil that would otherwise be lost. It is also a very convenient way of getting rid of waste. There are environmental benefits, too, as composting recycles material that would otherwise find its way to landfill sites. Producing your own compost will save you money, because it means you need to buy less organic matter to improve your garden soil.

To compost successfully and efficiently you need the right equipment and an understanding of the principles of the decomposition process. Although you can compost organic waste perfectly well in a loose heap, it looks untidy and tends to decompose unevenly unless carefully managed. In most gardens a compost bin is a far better option.

WHAT TO COMPOST

A wide range of organic material from both the garden and household can be composted including (clockwise, from top left) most kitchen waste, weeds, shredded prunings and grass clippings.

Ideally, a bin should contain at least 1 cubic metre (about 30 cubic feet) of waste to allow it to heat up adequately and compost material quickly. The bin can be a simple structure made from old pallets nailed together to form a box or a neater home-made version fashioned from second-hand, tanalized fencing timber. Do not use untreated timber because it will rot along with the

A bonus crop

After the compost has been turned in the compost bin you can use it to grow a bonus crop of vegetables. Simply cover the top of the compost with about 15cm (6in) of garden soil and plant hungry vegetables, such as marrows (large zucchini), pumpkins or cucumbers. They will benefit from the heat generated by the decomposing compost and the extra nutrients made available.

contents. Alternatively, you can buy a ready-made compost bin, but make sure you choose one that will hold sufficient organic waste. The compost should be easily accessible when it is ready to use.

What can you compost?

Almost all organic waste material from the garden and household can be recycled, but to decompose quickly and form a crumbly, sweet-smelling, fibrous material, the right ingredients must be combined. Ideally, add dry material, such as prunings, old newspapers and straw, with equal quantities of green, wet

HOW TO MAKE COMPOST

1 A simple compost bin, which should be about 1m (3ft) square, can be made using cheap, pressure-treated fencing timber, or by nailing four flat pallets together.

2 Pile the waste into the bin, taking care that there are no thick layers of the same material. Grass clippings, for example, will not rot down if the layer is too thick because the air cannot penetrate.

3 It is important to keep the compost bin covered with an old mat or a sheet of polythene (sheet vinyl or plastic). This will help to keep in the heat generated by the rotting process and will also prevent the compost from getting too wet in bad weather.

organic waste, such as grass clippings. Before adding to the compost heap, make sure that dry and woody material is chopped finely with secateurs (pruners) or a garden shredder. Do not add meat, fish, fat or other cooked foods to the compost bin because they will attract vermin. Also throw away perennial weed roots and annual weeds that are setting seed because these may survive the composting process.

Mix up the material before adding it to the compost bin or add the material in layers no more than 15cm (6in) deep.

Speeding up composting

There are several actions you can take to minimize the time it takes for the composting process to be completed. Give the decomposition process a kick-start by adding a proprietary compost activator or a spadeful of well-rotted compost from a previous bin to each layer of material added. This will provide extra nitrogen and introduce the necessary micro-organisms needed for decomposition. Fill the bin as quickly as you can so that there is

sufficient organic material to heat up and decompose quickly. Make sure that the material is moist enough when it is added. Check after a few weeks to see if it has dried out and water if necessary.

So the material does not get too wet, cover it with a lid, piece of old carpet or sheet of plastic. If the compost does get too wet, turn out the bin and mix in more dry material before refilling the bin. Insulate the bin in winter with bubble polythene or old carpet so that the core of the heap does not cool down. Turn the decomposing organic matter after about a month so that the material on the outside is placed in the centre of the bin. This will introduce air and produce a more uniform compost at the end of the process. After about two months in summer and up to six months in winter the compost should be ready to use.

Making leafmould

Autumn leaves are another source of useful organic matter. If you have a small garden, fill black plastic bags with leaves, add a little water if the leaves are dry and seal by knotting

Chicken wire attached to four wooden posts makes an ideal container for autumn leaves. The leafmould can be used on the garden after about a year.

the top. Puncture a few holes in the sides with a garden fork to allow air in before putting the bags in an out-of-the-way place, such as behind the shed. The leaves take about a year to break down into a rich, crumbly texture, which can then be used on the garden. Speed the process by adding a few handfuls of grass clippings to each bag before sealing.

In a large garden make a special enclosure with chicken wire and corner posts. Cover with carpet to prevent the leaves from blowing away.

4 After about a month, turn the contents of the compost bin with a fork to let in air and to move the outside material, which is slow to rot, into the centre to speed up the rotting process. If you have several bins, it is easier to turn the compost from one bin into another.

5 When the bin is full, you may want to cover the surface with a layer of soil and use it to grow marrows (large zucchini), pumpkins or cucumbers. If you want to use the contents as soon as possible, omit the soil and keep the compost covered with plastic.

Compost

Good garden compost is dark brown, fibrous and crumbly. It has a sweet earthy smell, not a rotting one. Compost can be used straight away or left covered until required.

Choosing and using fertilizers

Plants need a range of essential nutrients to grow well. The amount of fertilizer you use and how often you need to apply it will depend on your soil and the types of crops you are trying to grow.

Essential nutrients

In nature a nutritional cycle occurs whereby plants take nutrients from the soil as they grow, then eventually die and rot, allowing the nutrients to return to the soil. In the garden you can mimic this process to some extent by recycling all your organic waste in a compost bin and using the compost to return nutrients to the soil. A proportion of the organic matter is not returned, however, so the soil needs replenishment from other sources. Fertilizers are a convenient method of providing the nutrients that are needed for healthy growth. Your choice will depend on the nutrients already available from your soil and the type of growth you want to encourage.

There are three macro- or primary nutrients, nitrogen (N), phosphorus (P) and potassium (K), the proportions of which are expressed as a ratio of N:P:K on the labels of fertilizer packs. Each macro-nutrient promotes a different type of growth.

If they are to flower reliably year after year, perennials and shrubs, such as this camellia, should be given the nutrients they need. Fertilizer rich in potassium encourages good flower production.

Nitrogen This nutrient encourages leafy growth, so it is useful for adding to leafy crops such as spinach and cabbages.
Phosphorus An essential nutrient for healthy roots, phosphorus also promotes the ripening of fruit.
Potassium Available in the form of potash, this promotes flowering and good fruit production.

Three other nutrients, calcium, magnesium and sulphur, are needed in smaller quantities and are known as secondary nutrients, and seven more, boron, chlorine, copper, iron, manganese, molybdenum and zinc, are also essential but in very small amounts. These are known as micronutrients or trace elements.

Types of fertilizer

Fertilizers are grouped according to their mode of manufacture or origin. Organic fertilizers are derived from naturally occurring organic materials, such as animals and plants. Some of the most widely used are bonemeal (high in phosphorus), fishmeal, fish,

HOW TO ADD ORGANIC MATERIAL

1 Organic material such as well rotted garden compost or farmyard manure is high in nutrients. Fork in when the soil is dug. For heavy soils this is best done in the autumn.

2 If the soil has already been dug, the organic material can be lightly forked in or left on the surface. The worms will complete the task of working it into the soil.

3 In autumn, and again in spring, top-dress established plants with a layer of well-rotted organic material.

INORGANIC FERTILIZERS   **ORGANIC FERTILIZERS**

balanced general fertilizer   sulphate of ammonia   blood   bonemeal

potash   superphosphate   seaweed   fish, blood and bone

blood and bone, hoof and horn (high in nitrogen) and seaweed meal (also high in nitrogen). They are slow acting because they have to be broken down by micro-organisms in the soil before the nutrients they contain become available to plants. The rate of breakdown of the fertilizer varies according to the prevailing conditions: if it is warm and moist breakdown speeds up; when it is cold or dry it slows down. Nutrients are thus released when plants need them most and are growing strongly. For these reasons organic fertilizers are acceptable to most organic growers.

Inorganic fertilizers are man-made. Most are manufactured, but a few, such as rock potash, are naturally occurring minerals that are mined. They are concentrated and usually quick acting because they are soluble in water so are immediately available to the plants. Although effects can be immediate, such fertilizers are easily leached from the soil by heavy rains, especially in winter and on well-drained soil.

These fertilizers can be further grouped according to the amount of N, P and K they contain. As the name suggests, balanced fertilizers (also known as complete fertilizers) contain an equal proportion of each macro-nutrient, an N:P:K of 7:7:7 being typical. Specific fertilizers, on the other hand, have different ratios of N:P:K. They are usually sold labelled as beneficial for particular plants, such as lawns or roses. Straight or simple fertilizers are the final group and these supply just one of the macro-nutrients, such as superphosphate (phosphorus), or potassium sulphate (potassium).

To make selection even more complicated, some fertilizers are supplied in combination with other chemicals, such as a fungicide, insecticide or herbicide. They are a convenient but usually an expensive way of buying fertilizer.
Slow-release fertilizers are inorganic fertilizers that have been coated in a special resin so that the nutrients are released slowly over time. They

mimic organic fertilizers in that they release more nutrients when the soil is warm and moist, just when the plants need it.

You can buy slow-release fertilizers that will last from a few weeks to the whole season. Because they cannot be washed away they are particularly suited for use in containers that are regularly watered throughout the growing season.

Fertilizers are also available in liquid formulations. Liquid growmore or liquid seaweed extract will promote general plant growth, but a high-potash feed, such as rose or tomato fertilizer, will encourage flowers and the formation of fruit.

Foliar feeds

Dilute fertilizer solutions can be applied to, and absorbed through, the plants' foliage. They are quick acting and useful for giving plants a boost part-way through the growing season or for correcting a deficiency.

Lawns

A lawn has a dramatic effect on the atmosphere of a garden. When it is kept neat and tidy it will greatly enhance the overall appearance as well as act as a calming visual counter-balance to busy and colourful beds and borders. If you have just moved into a new house the best way to get the garden started is to lay a new lawn. You do not have to worry about the size or shape at this stage because it can be easily changed later on when you have formulated your overall garden design.

When you design a new lawn it is important to keep the shape simple to reduce the time you will have to spend mowing and edging. Tight curves and corners might look dramatic, but they are awkward to cut. If the lawn runs right up to the base of a wall or fence consider installing a mowing edge so that you do not have to stop and trim wayward grass stems. An edging strip is also a good idea along borders, reducing maintenance time still further.

A long lawn draws the eye to the end of the garden. Rhododendrons spilling out on to the grass help soften the edges of the lawn.

Creating a new lawn

The decision to create a new lawn is not one to be taken lightly, but it does give you the opportunity to give your garden a top quality surface. A new lawn is best laid in spring or early autumn.

Seed or turf?

The main consideration once you have decided to have a new lawn is whether to grow it from seed or lay turf. Seed is cheaper, costing less than a quarter of the price of turf, and is easier to do. It is also more flexible because you can wait until the weather and soil conditions are just right. Turf, on the other hand, has to be put down almost as soon as it is delivered and is hard work to lay.

Preparing the ground

First dig over the area, clearing the ground of weeds, including the roots of perennials. If sowing seeds, leave for a week or two to allow any weed seeds to germinate. These will need to be killed using a weedkiller spray (choose a type that leaves the area safe for replanting within a few days) or by hoeing.

Creating a level surface

A few days after killing the surface weeds, rake the ground level using a soil rake and remove any stones or other debris that have come to the surface. Then tread the whole area using tiny shuffling steps with the weight on your heels. Repeat this process until an even, level and firm surface has been produced. It is worth investing the time and effort to create a perfectly level bed whether you are sowing seed or laying turf, as this will improve the appearance of your lawn later.

HOW TO SOW A NEW LAWN

1 Dig the ground thoroughly, removing deep-rooted perennial weeds. Rake the soil level. Use pegs marked with lines drawn 5cm (2in) down from the top as a guide, having checked with a spirit (carpenter's) level on a straightedge that the pegs are level.

2 Allow the soil to settle for a week, then consolidate it further by treading it evenly to remove large air pockets. The best way to do this is to shuffle your feet over the area, first in one direction then at right angles.

3 Rake the consolidated soil to produce a fine, crumbly structure suitable for sowing seeds. If you can, leave the area for a couple of weeks to allow weed seeds to germinate. Hoe them off or use a weedkiller that leaves the ground safe for replanting within days.

4 Use string to divide the area into strips a metre (yard) wide and divide the strips into squares with bamboo canes or stakes. Move the canes along the strips as you sow.

5 Use a small container that holds enough seed for a square metre (yard). Make a mark on it if the amount only partly fills the container. Scatter the seeds as evenly as possible with a sweeping motion of the hand.

6 Hire or buy a calibrated granular fertilizer spreader to sow large areas quickly. Check the delivery rate over sheets of paper first and adjust the spreader until the correct amount is being applied per square metre (yard).

HOW TO LAY A LAWN WITH TURFS

1 Dig and consolidate the soil as described for seed, but there is no need to leave it for a few weeks to allow weed seeds to germinate: the turf will prevent them from sprouting. Start by laying the turf along a straight edge.

2 Stand on a plank while you lay the next row, as this will distribute your weight. Stagger the joints between rows to create a bond like brickwork. Turf in a long roll will have fewer joints but again these should not align.

3 Tamp down each row of turf to eliminate air pockets with the head of a rake, then roll the plank forwards to lay the next row. Brush sandy soil, or a mixture of peat and sand, into the joints to help bind the turfs together.

Planting the lawn

A couple of days before laying turf or sowing seed, scatter a general fertilizer at the recommended rate over the area and rake lightly into the surface of the soil. If sowing seed, choose a windless day, preferably when rain is forecast and lightly rake the grass seed into the surface. It is a good idea to protect the area with fine mesh netting to keep off birds and cats.

For both seed and turf, keep the area well watered, if it does not rain heavily, until the grass is well established. For turf this should be about two weeks, for seed it will be considerably longer.

A good-quality lawn invites you into the garden, leading the eye smoothly to beds and borders. If your lawn is in very bad condition it is worth considering starting from scratch and sowing seed or laying turf to get the effect you want.

Looking after your lawn

A lawn needs regular mowing throughout the growing season. Other maintenance tasks such as removing moss and weeds, seasonal feeding and watering and other lawn treatments may also be necessary to keep it in tip-top condition.

Mowing and trimming

From the time the grass starts to grow in early spring it will need to be cut and trimmed regularly until the end of the growing season. The first spring cut should be made when the lawn is dry after the grass reaches about 8cm (3in) long. Brush off any wormcasts before you mow. Make sure the blades of the mower are set high so that they trim off just a couple of centimetres (less than 1in). Gradually lower the cutting height over the next few mows until it is cutting the grass back to 4cm (1½in). Collect lawn clippings from the early cuts. Thereafter, mow the lawn every time the grass has grown about 2cm (¾in). You do not need a grass box to collect the clippings if you mow this often because they can be left on the lawn as a mulch, returning nutrients to the soil.

Controlling moss

A lawn that contains a lot of moss should be treated by applying a specially formulated moss killer to the grass in the autumn or spring. Use a treatment recommended for the season. The mixture known as lawn sand, sometimes used to kill moss, is fine in spring, but it contains too much nitrogen for autumn use. Moss is fairly easy to eliminate using a lawn treatment, but to achieve long-term control you need to tackle the underlying causes that encourage moss. A lawn becomes colonized by moss because the grass is not growing vigorously enough. This could be due to poor drainage, too much shade or soil that is too acidic – if you are unsure, check it using a simple pH kit. Where shade is the problem, thin out any overhanging branches of trees or cut back shrubs.

Killing weeds

Isolated weeds can be removed with an old kitchen knife or treated using a spot weedkiller. You may need to treat areas of established perennial weeds several times to kill them completely. Where the problem is more widespread use an overall lawn treatment. On a small lawn apply a granular weedkiller using a hand shaker pack or apply a liquid weedkiller using a watering can fitted with a weedkiller dribble bar. Large lawns are quicker and easier to treat by applying a granular weedkiller using a calibrated fertilizer spreader. Coarse grass weeds can also spoil the appearance of a lawn and are not affected by lawn weedkillers. You can either dig out the coarse grasses by hand and reseed the bare patch, or weaken the weed grass over time by slashing through the patches with a sharp knife each time you mow.

HOW TO REMOVE WEEDS

1 Use a special weeding tool or a knife to prise up single weeds. Push the tool in next to the root and lift the plant out with a lever action as you pull with the other hand. Even deep-rooted plants can be removed like this.

2 Widespread weeds are best controlled by a selective weedkiller, ideally in spring. They are usually applied as a liquid, using a dribble bar attached to a watering can. Always mix and apply as recommended by the manufacturer.

3 If there are just a few troublesome weeds, spot treatment may be a more economical and quicker method. Brush or dab on a selective weedkiller. Be careful not to kill the grass as well as the weeds.

4 Make any necessary lawn repairs. If you have had to lift a lot of weeds growing close together, leaving a bare patch in your lawn, sprinkle grass seeds over the area.

FEEDING YOUR LAWN

If your lawn is in poor condition and needs reviving, apply a lawn feed. Choose one formulated for the season: spring and summer feeds have much more nitrogen than autumn feeds.

If you want your lawn to remain green all summer, you will have to water it regularly during dry spells. A water sprinkler takes much of the hard work out of this tedious task.

Feeding and watering

A vigorously growing lawn is less likely to be colonized by weeds and mosses. Keep the grass growing strongly by ensuring it receives plenty of water in long, dry spells. Apply a high-nitrogen lawn feed once a year in spring and use a slow-release formulation feed throughout the growing season. If you also have a problem with moss or weeds use a combined lawn weed and feed, or lawn weed, feed and moss killer.

Clearing the lawn

Where there is no obvious sign of moss but the lawn still feels spongy when you walk on it, the problem is likely to be the build-up of dead grass stems at the base of the lawn, known as thatch. When the thatch gets more than 1cm (⅛in) thick it starts to suffocate the lawn and must be removed, a technique known as scarifying. Use a spring-tine or wire lawn rake and vigorously rake out the thatch. This is hard work, so if you have a large area to deal with it is worth considering buying or hiring a powered lawn rake to do the job. Scarify your lawn thoroughly once a year in autumn.

Falling leaves also cause a problem and must be removed, otherwise the grass beneath will turn yellow from lack of light and be prone to disease.

HOW TO REMOVE THATCH

Grass clippings, leaves and other debris form a thatch at the base of grasses in your lawn which can stifle them. Remove it with a spring-tine rake. Raking also removes moss.

HOW TO COLLECT LEAVES

1 Don't let autumn leaves lie on your lawn for long or the grass underneath will suffer. Clear the leaves up with a lawn rake.

2 Rake the leaves into piles and scoop them up with a pair of short planks (boards). Choose a still day when the leaves are dry to make the job pleasant.

Repairing your lawn

Many lawns receive a lot of wear, especially during the summer months. Fortunately, the autumn is an ideal time to make repairs. Use the following techniques to tackle humps and hollows, badly draining soil, bare patches, broken edges and areas that are simply worn out.

Bumps and hollows

When an uneven lawn is cut the high points will show up as light green because the grass is being cut too short and the low points as dark green patches. If the problem is widespread, you would be better off topdressing the whole lawn, but if you have just a few isolated bumps or hollows you can cure them using the following technique. Use a sharp spade or half-moon edging tool to make an H-shaped cut in the lawn centred over the bump or hollow. Carefully undercut the turf either side working from the central cut and peel back the turf to expose the soil beneath. Then either remove sufficient soil to level the bump when the turf is relaid, or top up with fine soil if you are levelling a hollow. Fill any gaps with an equal-parts mixture of sieved garden soil and sharp sand.

Repairing any broken edges will give your beds and borders a neat finish, essential when the impact of your garden design relies on straight lines.

Bare patches

Repair any bare patches in the lawn by using a garden fork to scratch the surface and gently loosen the soil. Then incorporate a general fertilizer such as growmore at the rate of 50g (2oz) per square metre (yard), before firming with the back of a soil rake. Sow grass seed over the top at the rate of about 35g (1½oz) per square metre (yard) for really bare patches and about 20g (1oz) per square metre (yard) if over-sowing sparse areas. Cover the seed

Aeration

Surface drainage can be impeded if the grass has become compacted because of excessive wear. You can overcome this by a technique known as aeration. Small areas are best treated with a garden fork. Simply spike it into the grass, pushing the tines into the ground to a depth of about 15cm (6in), spacing the holes about 5cm (2in) apart. For larger areas of lawn consider hiring a powered spiker or slitter instead. Fill the holes with sharp sand or a mixture of soil and sand for poorly drained soils, or use peat or very fine, well-rotted compost if the ground is sandy. Autumn is the best time to aerate your lawn.

1 If the grass growth is poor this could be because the soil is poorly drained. Aerate the lawn by pushing the prongs of a fork into the ground.

2 Gently brush a soil improver, such as sharp sand or a mixture of soil and sand, into the holes made by the fork.

with a light scattering of sieved garden soil and then water with a fine-rosed watering can. Protect the area from birds and cats by covering with a piece of garden fleece, held down with stones. Water again during dry spells until the new grass is well established.

Heavy wear

Areas that receive constant wear, such as under children's play equipment or at the bottom of steps on to a lawn, need to be reinforced if they are going to cope. If the lawn is used as a shortcut to another part of the garden consider incorporating stepping stones to take the impact. Where children's play equipment cannot be moved to spread the wear and tear around, reinforce the grass with heavy-duty plastic mesh. Cut the grass short, then peg the mesh down over the area so that it is held completely flat. Allow the grass to grow up through the mesh over the winter. When you come to mow next spring, the mesh will be hidden from sight, well below mower blade height so that you can mow straight over the top.

HOW TO RECUT AN EDGE

Insert a half-moon edging tool about 8cm (3in) into the soil. Lever the soil forwards to form a gulley with one vertical side against the lawn and one curved side against the border. Remove any grass to prevent it rooting.

HOW TO REPAIR A BROKEN EDGE

1 Use a half-moon edging tool or a spade to cut a rectangle around the affected area.

2 Push a spade under the rectangle, starting from the broken edge. Keep the thickness of the slice of grass as even as possible.

3 Reverse the turf so that the undamaged part of the turf is against the edge of the bed and the broken edge is within the lawn. Fill the hole caused by the damage with sifted soil and firm it down well.

4 Brush soil into the joints to help the grass knit together quickly and water well. Sow grass seed in the patched area, matching the type of grass if possible. Cover until the seed has germinated.

Broken edges

Isolated broken edges on lawns, perhaps caused by a careless heel or spade, are easy to repair. Use a sharp spade or half-moon edging tool to cut out a square at the edge of the lawn that encloses the damaged area. Undercut the turf and then turn it around 180 degrees so that the broken area is within the lawn and the straight part aligns with the edge of the lawn. Top up the damaged area with sieved garden soil if necessary, then level and firm with the back of a soil rake. Reseed as described for bare patches (above).

If the lawn is broken and uneven all along the edge of a border it is worth re-cutting to improve the appearance of your garden. Mark out where you will re-cut, using a board as a guide for straight edges or a length of garden hose for curved ones. Insert a sharp spade or half-moon edging tool into the soil. Lever back the handle and push the soil forwards to form a gulley with one vertical side against the lawn and one curved side against the border. Remove any unwanted grass to prevent it rooting into the border and becoming a weed problem.

Reducing maintenance time

The shape of a lawn – whether square, rectangular or irregular – will have a great influence on the amount of time it takes to keep it neat as well as the style of garden you are trying to create.

Lawn size

Obviously the larger a lawn the more time it will take to mow. This can, however, be offset somewhat by choosing a mower with a cutting width to match the size of your lawn. For a large lawn – more than 250 square metres (300 sq yards) – look for a mower with a cutting width of at least 35cm (14in). If you have a small lawn – less than 50 square metres (60 sq yards) – a mower with a cutting width of 25cm (10in) would be sufficient. A mower with a 30cm (12in) wide cut would be the best option for lawns in between these two extremes.

Wider mowers are usually more expensive, so consider whether the extra cost is worth it. The extra manoeuvrability of a smaller mower might be better in a smaller garden, with fewer straight runs.

Naturalizing bulbs in the lawn gives you a good excuse to leave the grass uncut.

The shape of the lawn

You can reduce the time and effort involved when mowing by keeping the shape of your lawn simple. Simple shapes often look more appealing than complicated fussy ones in any case. If your existing design has obstacles, such as island beds and specimen trees, you could reduce the amount of stopping and starting as well as the length of edge to be trimmed by joining the beds together or extending borders from the sides to incorporate them.

HOW TO CREATE A MOWING EDGE

1 A mowing edge of bricks or paving slab will prevent overhanging flowers smothering the edge of the lawn. Mark out the area of grass to be lifted using the paving as a guide. To keep the new edge straight, use a half-moon edger against the paving. Then lift the grass to be removed by slicing it off with a spade.

2 Remove enough soil to allow for the depth of the slab or brick and make a firm base by compacting gravel or a mixture of sand and gravel where the paving is to be laid. Use a plank of wood to make sure it is level. Allow for the thickness of the paving and a few blobs of mortar.

3 It is best to bed the edging on mortar for stability, but because it will not be taking a heavy weight, just press the slabs on to blobs of mortar and tap level with a mallet. The slabs should be laid evenly and flush with, or very slightly below, the lawn. Use a spirit (carpenter's) level to double-check.

Saving time in repairing your lawn

Lawns on very light, sandy soils can soon lose their sharpness as the edges of beds and borders crumble away. Even on other soils the edges of a lawn may be damaged by an ill-placed foot. Repairing the edges of a lawn can be a time-consuming task – perhaps repeated every spring – but it is necessary if your garden uses formal beds as an integral part of the design. To reduce the need for repairs, you can install a mowing edge or an edging strip. Bear in mind, though, that a raised edging strip will make it difficult to mow right up to the edge of the bed. Weigh up whether a strong, attractive edging is worth the extra mowing time.

If you have more than one lawn in your garden, consider joining them into one. Small lawns in the front garden often take more time to look after than the main one at the back. You may be better off getting rid of the small lawn altogether and replacing it with an area of gravel.

Mowing edges

It is a good idea to create a mowing edge if your garden is bounded by a border. It will mean the grass always has a neat edge and you won't damage overhanging border plants when you mow. On a large lawn the edging can be wide, especially if you have large, trailing plants that are likely to flop over the edge of the bed. If the lawn is small, however, use narrow edging so that it will look in proportion with the rest of the garden.

Cutting to different heights

If you have a large lawn consider leaving part of it to grow longer between cuts so that your workload is reduced. Keep broad "pathways" cut regularly, cut other areas with the blade set higher, and mow only every second or third time. Some areas can remain uncut except for a couple of times a season, which will allow wildflowers to thrive. Do bear in mind that very long grass cannot be cut with a standard mower and you will have to use a nylon-line trimmer or hire a powered scythe.

HOW TO FIT AN EDGING STRIP

1 Make a slit trench along the lawn edge with a spade, then lay the strip alongside the trench and cut to length. Place the edging strip loosely into the trench.

2 Backfill with soil for a firm fit. Press the strip in gently as you proceed. Finish off by tapping it level with a hammer over a straight-edged piece of wood.

HOW TO FIT WOODEN EDGING

Cut the roll to length using strong pliers to cut the wires and insert the edging in a narrow trench. Join the pieces by wiring them together. Backfill with soil for a firm fit. Use a hammer over a piece of wood to tap it down. Use a spirit (carpenter's) level to check the edging is level.

A mowing edge will lessen your work on a lawn, as the mower can get right up to the edge of the bed. You may have to trim any spreading grass stems, but this will only be necessary occasionally.

Planting in and around the lawn

Adding plants to your lawn can transform the appearance of your garden. Bulbs and wildflowers will provide seasonal interest, while trees and shrubs will add height and structure. Bear in mind that the more obstacles you place in the lawn the longer it will take to mow and trim, and you will break up the sweep of an uncluttered lawn.

Naturalized bulbs

In the wild, bulbs naturally form dramatic flowering drifts of colour under trees. This effect can be reproduced in the garden by planting bulbs in a natural-looking style. Early spring bulbs are a particularly good choice because they not only give a spectacular show but will be

out of the way before mowing starts in earnest. You need to wait six weeks after flowering before mowing the naturalized area. If you want to grow later-flowering bulbs this way, you would be better off creating a wildflower meadow, which does not need cutting until late summer.

To get a natural distribution of bulbs, toss them gently on to the lawn and plant them where they land. Clumps of bulbs are best planted by removing a whole turf with a sharp spade, planting at the correct depth, firming the soil and then replacing the turf. If you use this method, make sure you maintain the informal arrangement of the bulbs. Individual bulbs can be planted using a cylindrical bulb planter. If you are

Bulbs to naturalize in grass

Camassia	Galanthus
Chionodoxa	Leucojum
Colchicum	Muscari
Crocus	Narcissus
Erythronium	Ornithogalum
Fritillaria	Scilla

planting many bulbs, choose a model with a long handle and foot bar, which can be used like a spade. Push the planter vertically into the soil and remove a core that is deep enough for the bulb being planted. After positioning the bulb replace the core and carefully tread level. Bulbs susceptible to rot should be planted on gravel to improve drainage.

HOW TO NATURALIZE BULBS IN A LAWN

1 If you have a lot of small bulbs to plant in a limited area, try lifting an area of turf. Use a spade or half-moon edging tool to make an H-shaped cut.

2 Slice beneath the grass with a spade until you can fold back the turf for planting. Try to keep the spade level so the soil removed is an even thickness.

3 Loosen the ground, as it will be very compacted. If you want to apply a slow-acting fertilizer, such as bonemeal, work it into the soil at the same time.

4 Avoid planting in rows or regimented patterns. You want the bulbs to look natural and informal, so scatter them and plant where they fall.

5 Use a trowel or a bulb planter for large bulbs, making sure the bulb will be covered with twice its own depth of soil when the grass is returned.

6 Firm the soil then return the grass. Firm again if necessary to make sure it is flat, and water well. Water the grass again in dry weather.

7 Special bulb planters can be used for large bulbs. The planters remove a cylindrical core of soil.

8 Place the bulb at the bottom of the hole on a bed of gravel to improve drainage, if necessary, and replace the plug of earth.

HOW TO PLANT A LAWN TREE

1 Mark a circle 60–120cm (2–4ft) in diameter, using a trail of sand. Lift the grass, removing about 15cm (6in) of soil at the same time.

2 Insert a stake on the side of the prevailing wind. Place off-centre in the hole to allow the rootball to occupy the central position.

3 Check that the hole is deep enough for the rootball by placing the potted tree in the hole. After planting, the soil should be level with the original soil-mark on the trunk.

4 Replace the soil in layers, firming carefully with the heel of your boot as you go. Secure the tree to the stake, and then water well. Mulch the bed to suppress weeds.

Creating wildlife habitats

The number of flowers growing wild is diminishing. One way of helping is to create a wildflower garden. A massed display of native flowers looks wonderful, and provides a haven for native insects such as butterflies.

Wildflower meadow

The easiest way to create a wild-flower meadow is to sow it like a lawn using a special wildflower and grass mix. You can convert an existing lawn by clearing patches and sowing a wildflower seeds mixture, or by planting pot-grown species directly into the grass.

Feed meadows or lawns containing wildflowers in spring, but use an autumn formulation lawn feed which contains less nitrogen than spring formulations, reducing grass growth.

The meadow will need cutting just twice a year: once in early spring and the second time in mid- to late-summer after the flowers have seeded. Small areas can be cut using a nylon-line trimmer, but larger areas are more easily cut with a powered scythe, which can be bought or hired.

Trees and shrubs

The grass underneath a tree or shrub in a lawn is often of poor quality. Its leaves block the light while they are on the tree and suffocate the grass when they fall in the autumn. Specimen trees and shrubs are best grown in a bed cut into the grass.

HOW TO SOW AND PLANT WILDFLOWERS

1 The most satisfactory way to create a wildflower meadow is to sow a special mixture of wildflower seeds. Remember to completely clear the ground of all perennial weeds before you start.

2 To bury the seeds, simply rake in one direction and then in the other. It does not matter if some seeds remain on the surface. Keep the area well watered until the seeds germinate. Protect from birds if necessary.

3 For a very small area, wildflower plants may be more convenient. You can raise your own from seed or buy them. Plant into bare ground or in an existing lawn. Keep the plants well watered until established.

Water and rock gardening

Water features add a new dimension to your garden, providing colour, movement and gentle sound, which can be used to create a relaxing atmosphere. If well planned and given the right setting, water features are easy to look after and a joy to behold.

The most important consideration when creating a water feature is to site it correctly. It needs a sunny, open position well away from overhanging trees and dense shade. Choose a type of pond that complements the style of your garden and position it where it will be most appreciated.

When creating a pond, consider adding other complementary features to your garden at the same time. A bog garden blurs the divide between pond and garden and allows you to grow some wonderful plants, while a rock garden can be as natural or as dramatic as you like.

The purple flowers of *Iris sibirica* make a striking edging to a charming and informal garden pond.

Small water features

No contemporary garden would be complete without introducing water somewhere in the design. With modern equipment, small water features are easy to install.

Choosing a feature

Creating a water feature used to require considerable planning and some serious excavation, but the development of easy-to-install kits and reliable low-voltage submersible pumps means that even a novice can build an attractive, working feature in less than a day. Of course, careful planning is advisable to avoid errors, but once you have decided on a suitable position, the time required to install a water feature is short.

There is a huge range of features to choose from, but they can be grouped according to their function: a watercourse, which creates a stream effect; spouts, where a jet of water spills from a wall mask; gurgle ponds, where a water spout splashes over a feature such as a heap of pebbles; and still-water pools.

Bear in mind that the temperature of a small pond, situated in a suntrap, may fluctuate too much for fish to thrive.

Moving water features

All small features with moving water have the same basic equipment: a submersible pump and a reservoir to hold the water. The reservoir can be bought for the purpose or made from anything that holds water, from an inexpensive central-heating header tank to a hole lined with flexible pond liner. The reservoir needs only to be deep enough to completely cover the pump with water, but larger reservoirs are much easier to maintain because they require topping up less frequently, especially in summer.

HOW TO MAKE A PEBBLE FOUNTAIN

1 Mark out the diameter of the reservoir and dig a hole slightly wider and deeper than its dimensions. Place a shallow layer of sand at the bottom. Ensure the reservoir rim is slightly below the level of the surrounding soil.

2 Backfill the gap between the reservoir and the sides of the hole with soil. Firm in. Create a catchment area by sloping the surrounding soil slightly towards the rim of the reservoir. Place two bricks at the bottom to act as a plinth for the pump. Then position the pump.

3 Ensure the pipe used for the fountain spout will be 5–7cm (2–3in) higher than the sides of the reservoir. Line the catchment area with a plastic sheet and either cut it so the plastic drapes into the reservoir, or cut a hole in the centre for the fountain pipe. Fill with water.

4 Position the plastic sheet over the reservoir, with the fountain pipe protruding through the hole and fit the fountain spout.

5 Place a piece of galvanized mesh (large enough to rest on the rim of the reservoir) on top to support the weight of large wet cobbles. If you are using small stones, place a smaller mesh on top of the larger one to prevent them falling through.

6 Cover the area around the pump with a layer of cobbles. Check the height of the spout is satisfactory. When you are happy with the fountain, finish arranging the cobbles.

The finished gurgle fountain gives interest to what would otherwise have been a neglected corner of the garden.

Plants for miniature ponds

Acorus gramineus 'Variegatus'
Azolla filiculoides
Dwarf water lilies
Eichhornia crassipes
Juncus effusus f. *spiralis*
Marsilea quadrifolia
Trapa natans

What size pump?

The size of pump you require will depend on the amount of water needed to produce the effect you want. A small water feature will require a pump with a flow rate of about 450 litres (about 120 gallons) per hour, while a large fountain will need one that can supply 650 litres (about 170 gallons). If you want to combine features or have a watercourse you will need a much larger pump (see product packaging for details).

HOW TO PLANT A MINIATURE POND

Choose an attractive watertight container such as a sturdy bucket and fill it with water. Plant with dwarf or miniature varieties of *Nymphaea* (water lily) and *Eichhornia crassipes* (water hyacinth).

The easiest way to create a small water feature with moving water is to sink a reservoir into the ground so that it is about 5cm (2in) below the surrounding soil. Then create a catchment area for the feature by sloping the soil around the hole towards the reservoir, so that when it is lined with heavy-duty polythene or a flexible pond liner, water will drain back into the reservoir. Position the pump in the reservoir and cover with heavy-duty steel mesh and smaller mesh to prevent smaller pebbles from falling through. Arrange cobbles and pebbles on the mesh to hide the reservoir and the catchment area to create a pebble fountain.

You can change the display by adding a millstone or another focal point, or by adding different types of fountain jet on the outlet pipe of the pump to create all manner of display fountains.

Alternatively, use a piece of pipe to connect the outlet pipe to a wall mask or a free-standing waterspout.

Still patio pools

You can create a small attractive pool from a half-barrel or large bucket. Sink it into the ground or stand it on the patio as a raised pool. If the container is not properly sealed, line it with flexible pond liner, stapling the top edge just out of sight below the rim. Trim carefully to neaten the edges and cover the bottom with a layer of gravel. Fill with water and allow to stand for a few days before planting with dwarf pond plants such as dwarf water lilies, corkscrew rush and the variegated form of the Japanese rush.

Larger raised pools are available in kit form from garden retailers or they can be made from fibreglass liners supported with brick walls.

Making a pond

After deciding on the best position for a pond in your garden, you need to consider its style and dimensions as well as the construction materials.

Planning a pond

A self-sustaining pond that does not require constant maintenance should be as big as possible. Whatever the shape, it should have at least 5 square metres (over 50 square feet) of surface area, and so that it doesn't heat up too quickly in summer or get too cold in winter it also needs to be at least 60cm (24in) deep over much of that area. A marginal shelf 23cm (9in) wide and about 15cm (6in) below the surface of the water around the edge is needed to accommodate plants that like their roots in water but their shoots and leaves in the air. Before excavating, check that there are no underground obstructions, such as pipes and cables.

Lining a pond

A pond can be made with a rigid, pre-formed liner or with a special flexible liner. Rigid liners are usually made from plastic or fibreglass and

A brick or paved edge creates a fairly formal effect, but the pond has been made more interesting by using the excavated soil to build up a raised bed behind it.

they come in a range of shapes and sizes to suit most styles of garden. Rigid liners tend to be on the small side, with little space for marginal plants, and are more work to install. A flexible liner, made from PVC, butyl rubber or heavy-duty polythene, gives you a lot more control over the design of your

pond. It can be pleated at the corners to fit a rectangular or square-shaped pond, and it is particularly suitable for an informal pond because it can be folded to fit any shape you want. It does, however, require some skill to create a convincing shaped pond, and the liner can be easily damaged, especially on stony soil.

HOW TO INSTALL A FLEXIBLE LINER

1 Mark out the shape of the pond with garden hose or rope for curves and pegs and string for straight edges, then remove any turf and start to excavate the pond. Redistribute the topsoil to other parts of the garden.

2 Dig the whole area to about 23cm (9in) deep, then mark the positions of the marginal shelves. Each should be about 23cm (9in) wide. Dig the deeper areas to 50–60cm (20–24in) deep. Angle all the vertical sides so they slope slightly inwards.

3 Check the level as you work. Correct discrepancies using sieved garden soil. Make sure there are no sharp stones on the base and sides that might damage the liner, then line the hole with builders' sand.

What size flexible liner?

Flexible liners are available in a range of sizes. To calculate the size you will need for your pond, use the following formula:

Length = 2 x maximum depth + maximum length of the pond

Width = 2 x maximum depth + maximum width of the pond

For example, a pond that is 3 x 2m (10 x 6ft) with a maximum depth of 50cm (20in) will require a flexible liner that is 4 x 3m (13⅓ x 9⅓ft).

Edging the pond

The style of edging and the material used should reflect the formality of the pond and the materials used elsewhere in the garden. A formal pond looks best with a neat, straight edge of paving, while an informal one can be paved with irregularly shaped stones or small unit paving, which can follow the gentle curves of the pond. Around the edge of a wildlife pond, a sloping pebble beach would be appropriate so that visiting wildlife can enjoy a bathe and a drink.

HOW TO INSTALL A PRE-FORMED RIGID LINER

1 Transfer the shape to the ground by inserting canes around the edge of the unit. Use a garden hose, rope or sand to mark the outline on the ground.

2 Remove the unit and canes and excavate the hole to approximately the required depth, following the profile of the shelves as accurately as possible.

3 Use a spirit (carpenter's) level and straight-edged board, laid across the rim, to check it is level. Measure down to check that it is the required depth.

4 Remove any large stones. Put the pond in the hole, then add or remove soil to ensure a snug and level fit. Check with a spirit level that the pond is level.

5 Remove the pond and line the hole with damp sand if the soil is stony. With the pond in position and levels checked again, backfill with sand or fine soil, being careful not to push the pond out of level.

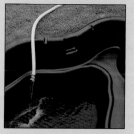
6 Fill with fresh water and backfill further if necessary as the water level rises, checking the level frequently to make sure the liner has not moved. Allow to stand for a few days before stocking with plants.

4 On stony soil, you may need to line the hole further with loft insulation or special pond liner underlay. Trim the liner underlay so that it fits neatly into the hole.

5 Ease the liner into position without stretching it unduly. Choose a warm day because this will make it more flexible. Weigh down the edges with stones, then fill the pond slowly. Ease the liner into position so that it follows the contours as the pond fills.

6 Once the pond is full, trim back the excess liner to leave an overlap of at least 15cm (6in) around the edge. Cover the overlapping liner with paving or other edging. To disguise the liner, overlap the water's edge by 2.5cm (1in).

Stocking a pond

It is essential to choose the right blend of aquatic plants to create a natural balance in your pond. Select plants that suit the size of the pond so they don't need regular chopping back to keep them in check.

Types of water plant

Pond plants can be grouped according to the depth of water they require.

Deep-water plants These plants, which include *Nymphaea* (water lily), are essential to the overall health of the pond because the leaves cover the surface and provide shade, which discourages the growth of algae and offers a cool retreat for fish.

Marginal plants The roots of marginal plants are in water but the stems and leaves grow above the surface. Most flower for only a short time between late spring and late summer, so try to combine varieties with different flowering times to prolong the period of interest. In addition, include plants with attractive foliage, such as the variegated irises *I. pseudacorus*

An informal pool, where nature is allowed to have its way, will soon become a haven for wildlife.

'Variegata' or *I. laevigata* 'Variegata', or *Schoenoplectus lacustris* subsp. *tabernaemontani*, which lasts for months.

Submerged aquatic plants Although not as ornamental as other plants, submerged aquatics are important for keeping the pond healthy. They use up excess nutrients that would otherwise encourage blanketweed and other algae. They also oxygenate the

water, improving the environment for fish and other pond creatures. Add around ten bunches per square metre (yard) of pond surface area.

Free-floating plants These plants, together with those that live in deep water, provide shade for fish and discourage the growth of algae. Aim to cover about one-third of the surface area with floating foliage.

HOW TO PLANT AQUATICS

1 Fill a basket sold for water plants with special aquatic compost. The hessian (burlap) liner will help prevent the soil from falling through the mesh sides of the basket.

2 Remove the plant from its container and plant it in the basket at its original depth, using a trowel to add or remove aquatic compost as necessary. Firm it in well.

3 Cover the aquatic compost with gravel to help keep it in place when you put the container in the pond and to minimize disturbance by fish. Soak the plant in a bucket of water to remove air bubbles.

Planting

The easiest way to introduce an aquatic plant is to use a special planting basket. If you use one of the traditional mesh-sided baskets, line it with hessian (burlap) before planting so the compost does not wash out. The extra lining will not be necessary if you are using a modern micromesh aquatic basket. Use specially formulated aquatic compost because standard potting compost (soil mix) will allow nutrients to leach out, encouraging excessive algae growth. Good quality topsoil can also be used if you find it difficult to get aquatic compost.

Although you can put more than one plant in a large basket, you are better off planting singly so that individual plants can later be removed and divided or replaced more easily. Top the basket with a 2cm (½in) deep layer of pea gravel to stop fish disturbing the compost and muddying the water. Soak the basket in a bucket of water before positioning it in the pond.

4 Once thoroughly soaked, carefully place the plant on the shelf at the edge of the pool so that the container is covered by 3–5cm (1–2in) of water.

HOW TO PLANT AN OXYGENATOR

Submerged aquatic plants are called oxygenators and are essential for the health of the pond. To plant an oxygenator such as *Lagarosiphon major* (curly water thyme), tie it to a stone, then drop it in the water. The plant will root in the sediment at the bottom of the pool.

STOCKING A WILDLIFE POND

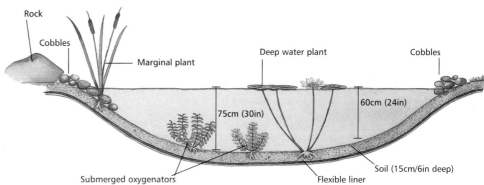

Rock
Cobbles
Marginal plant
Deep water plant
Cobbles
75cm (30in)
60cm (24in)
Submerged oxygenators
Flexible liner
Soil (15cm/6in deep)

This pool has a sloping edge to allow birds and animals to reach the water easily. Surround it with lush plantings and long grass to provide cover for visiting wildlife.

INTRODUCING FISH

Never place fish directly in the pond. First acclimatize them by floating the plastic bag that you transported them in on the surface of the water for an hour. This will allow the water temperatures to equalize gradually, after which the fish can be allowed to swim out of the bag.

Trouble-free pond plants

Deep-water plants
Nymphaea 'Attraction'
   N. 'Aurora'
   N. 'Ellisiana'
   N. 'Froebelii'
   N. 'Pygmaea Helvola'
Nymphoides peltata (water fringe)
Orontium aquaticum (golden club)

Marginal plants
Acorus calamus 'Variegatus'
Butomus umbellatus (flowering rush)
Caltha palustris 'Flore Pleno'
   (marsh marigold)
Iris laevigata 'Variegata'

Myosotis scorpioides
Pontederia cordata (pickerel weed)
Schoenoplectus lacustris
Typha minima

Submerged and floating plants
Azolla filiculoides (fairy moss)
Eichihornia crassipes (water hyacinth)
Eleocharis acicularis (hair grass)
Fontinalis antipyretica
Hydrocharis morsus-ranae
Ranunculus aquatilis
Stratiotes aloides (water soldier)
Trapa natans
Utricularia vulgaris

Pond care

Once established, a well-planned and constructed pond will largely look after itself. There are, however, a number of seasonal tasks worth carrying out that will help maintain the equilibrium.

A mature specimen of the water lily *Nymphaea* 'Attraction' in early summer.

Spring

Once the coldest weather is over, you can remove the netting keeping out wind-blown leaves and exchange the pond heater for a pump. The pond will come to life in mid-spring, when marginal plants put on new growth, the first lily pads appear and on a mild day fish can be seen at the surface. This is the time to start feeding the fish and to carry out a pond spring clean. Scoop any dead or rotting leaves from the pond to prevent them from fouling the water.

Mid- to late spring is an ideal time to add new plants to your pond. It is worth adding special fertilizer tablets to the compost of established plants. Make sure they are pushed well into the compost so that nutrients do not leach out into the water and encourage the growth of algae. If the pond tends to go green with algae at this time of year, place a barley straw pad (available from garden retailers) in the pond.

Summer

Choose a warm, fine day in late spring or early summer to remove and divide overgrown plants.

Fish will need feeding on a regular basis throughout summer. Try to feed in the morning and clear away any uneaten food left floating on the surface of the water after about 10 minutes using a fine-mesh fishing net. This will prevent it from sinking to the bottom and rotting.

Pond problems often occur in summer. Use a jet of water from a hose to knock off sap-sucking pests from water lily pads. Spreading filaments of blanketweed should be scooped out with a bamboo cane or wire rake. Before placing it on the compost heap, leave the weed on the side of the pond for a couple of hours to allow any pond creatures to make their way back into the pond. Use a fine-mesh net to scoop out floating duckweed, which can quickly spread over the surface of a pond. Top up the water level as necessary and clean the filter of the pump if there appears to be a blockage. In heavy, thundery weather you may

HOW TO DIVIDE A WATER LILY

1 Lift the water lily in spring, put it in a bowl of water and wash it free of compost. Trim back any over-long roots with secateurs (pruners) and remove any damaged leaves.

2 Using a sharp knife, cut the rhizome into pieces, making sure that each section has roots and leaves or leaf buds.

3 Pot the sections up into pots of aquatic compost. Add a layer of gravel to prevent the compost being disturbed. Put the pot in a bowl of water and keep it in a shaded place. New leaves will appear within a few months.

HOW TO OVERWINTER TENDER AQUATICS

1 Net a few plants in good condition. They may already be deteriorating in the cooler weather, so don't save any that appear to be rotting or badly damaged.

2 Put a handful of the plants in a plastic container of pond water. Don't overcrowd them – use extra containers rather than allow them to touch. Some gardeners put a little soil in the bottom to provide nutrients.

3 Keep the plants in a light, frost-free place, such as a greenhouse. You might be able to keep them on a cool windowsill. Top up or change the water occasionally so that it does not become stagnant.

see fish gasping for air at the surface. Increase oxygen levels in the water by turning on the pump or by playing a jet of water from a hose on to the surface.

Autumn

The main tasks of autumn are to clear away the dying foliage of marginal plants and to prevent leaves from nearby deciduous trees from falling into the pond. Cut down marginals so that the tops of their stems are above the water surface when the pond is full. Remove any other organic material. Place tender aquatics in a bucket of pond water

somewhere cool but frost free, such as a greenhouse, until spring. In early autumn use a high-protein fish food to help fish build up sufficient reserves to survive the winter, then when the weather cools stop feeding altogether. Remove the pond pump, store carefully and replace with a pool heater, which will help keep at least part of the water's surface ice free in freezing weather.

Winter

If you completed all the pond-care tasks on time in autumn, little needs to be done other than to keep the pond clear of fallen leaves that are

still blowing about the garden and to make sure that at least part of the pond's surface remains free of ice during prolonged cold weather.

The easiest way to clear an area of ice is to stand a pan of hot water on the surface to melt a hole. Never hit the ice with a hammer to try to break it up because this will send shock waves through the pond that can harm fish. If a substantial ice-sheet has formed on the pond, you could siphon off a couple of inches of water from underneath the ice. The layer of air will help to insulate the water and prevent any more water from freezing.

SUMMER MAINTENANCE

Submerged oxygenators, such as *Lagarosiphon major*, and rampant growers, such as *Myriophyllum aquaticum*, will clog the pond unless you clear them out periodically. Remove the excess with a net or rake.

HOW TO PREPARE A POND FOR WINTER

1 A small pond can be protected from the worst of the leaf fall with a fine-mesh net. Anchor it just above the surface of the pond. Remove the leaves regularly and eventually take the netting off.

2 If you cannot cover your pond with a net, use a fish net or rake to remove leaves regularly – not only from the surface but also from below the surface. Decomposing leaves in the pond will pollute the water.

Bog gardens

Marshy bog gardens associate particularly well with water features, helping to create a natural setting, but they are also worth considering as features in their own right because they allow you to grow a wider range of plants in your garden.

Deciding on a site

Bog gardens are areas of permanently wet soil that are suitable for growing marginal and wetland plants. They look particularly effective alongside water features, where the lush foliage and colourful flowers help to integrate pools into the rest of the garden. A bog garden can be either planted in a permanently water-logged area in your garden or created in a dry spot using a pond liner.

The soil in a bog garden must be kept moist, which may mean regular watering during the summer months. Before planting a bog garden consider installing a seep hose under the soil for automatic watering.

Creating a bog garden

A bog garden is very easy to create. If you are building a pond at the same time you can simply extend the excavation and use a single piece of flexible liner to line both the pond

CREATING A BOGGY MARGIN TO A POND

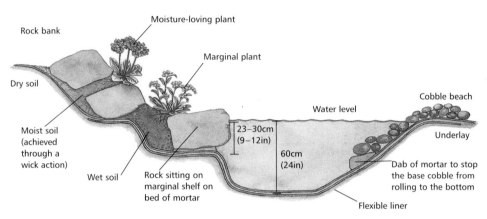

Adding a boggy margin to a pond will make it more attractive and help integrate it into the surrounding garden. It is the perfect spot to experiment with unusual moisture-loving plants.

and the bog area. However, you can also create a bog garden near to an existing water feature or make it a feature in its own right. Simply scoop out an area about 45cm (18in) deep with sloping sides and a flat base to the hole. Don't make it too small, otherwise the soil will be prone to drying out, but try to keep the widest part no more than 2m (6ft) across so that it will be easy to reach and maintain the plants in the centre. Line the hole with sand as you would a pond and then cover with a flexible liner.

If you are building the bog garden at the same time as the pond, make

a ridge of stones along the border between the two and lay some fine-mesh netting on the bog garden side along the inside of the stones. This will stop soil washing through the stones and muddying the pond. To allow excess water to drain away,

Good bog garden plants

Aruncus	Hosta
Astilbe	Iris
Caltha	Ligularia
Cardamine	Lysichiton
Filipendula	Lobelia (some)
Hardy ferns	Primula (some)
Hemerocallis	Zantedeschia

HOW TO PLANT A BOG PLANT

1 Adjust the position of the bog plants while they are still in their pots until you are satisfied with the arrangement. Water each container well and allow to drain before planting the centre of the bog garden first.

2 Make a planting hole slightly larger than the container and plant at the same depth. Firm the soil carefully around each plant.

3 Level the soil over the bog garden after planting is complete and cover the surface with a layer of loose organic mulch to help prevent moisture loss. Take care not to pile the mulch against the stems of the plants.

HOW TO PROPAGATE BOG PLANTS BY SEED

1 Fill the base of a seed tray with stones for drainage, then fill with aquatic compost to within 1cm (½in) of the top.

2 Firm down the aquatic compost with a tray of the same size, but do not compact it. Moisten the compost by standing the tray in shallow water for a couple of hours until the surface of the compost darkens with moisture.

3 Scatter the seeds thinly and cover with compost. Spray regularly to keep the compost moist. When they are big enough to handle, pot up the seedlings and grow them on.

make a few well-spaced holes in the bog garden liner and cover with a 5cm (2in) layer of grit. Trim the flexible liner to leave a 15cm (6in) overlap on all sides before filling the bog garden with a mixture of three parts topsoil to one part well-rotted organic matter. Allow the soil to settle for a couple of weeks and then mix in a slow-release fertilizer. Water well before planting up with your chosen bog plants. Start in the centre and work your way outwards. As a finishing touch, cover the liner flap with decorative pebbles or other stones. Alternatively, if it is next to a border, cover it with a thin layer of soil or mulch.

Careful planting of the bog garden will help to make a subtle transition to the wider garden.

Rock gardens

Like ponds or watercourses, rock gardens benefit from an open site. If planned well, they can each enhance the other. In a level garden the soil excavated during pond installation can be used to form the base.

Building a rock garden

When you build a rock garden, aim as far as possible to create as natural-looking outcrop, otherwise it will take on the appearance of a rock-encrusted heap of soil. The most important ingredient is the rocks, which are more likely to "gel" as a rocky outcrop if they are of the same natural stone. Choose a type of rock that has clear strata lines running through it and an attractive texture and colour. Limestone and sandstone are perhaps the best rock types, but it is possible to create an attractive feature from other types of rock.

You will need a range of sizes of rock – anything from 15kg (33lb) to 100kg (well over 200lb) – so make sure you have help to manoeuvre the larger stones. If you live near a quarry, use this as your source, otherwise suppliers can be found in local directories, and a limited selection of rocks is offered at some garden centres.

Rock gardens are perfect for growing a selection of alpine plants.

HOW TO BUILD A ROCK GARDEN

1 The base of the rock garden is a good place to dispose of rubble and subsoil excavated if you have dug out a pond.

2 Use a special soil mixture for the top 15–23cm (6–9in), especially if soil excavated from a pond is used. Mix equal parts of soil, coarse grit and peat (or peat substitute) and spread evenly over the mound.

3 Lay the first rocks at the base, making sure that the strata run in the same direction, and add more soil mixture around them.

Designing a rock garden

The design should suit the situation. On sloping ground you can build a natural-looking outcrop or a series of terraces or a combination of the two for a very large rockery. On a level site a more acute outcrop, with strata lines at a 45 degree angle, can work well, or choose a series of flattish stones to create a pavement effect with horizontal strata lines.

Careful planning is essential. Mark out the site using string and improve drainage if necessary – if you have heavy soil this may mean digging a hole 30cm (12in) deep, half-filling it with rubble and covering it with a layer of sharp sand before topping with good-quality, free-draining topsoil mixture.

Building a rockery on a slope

If practicable start at the bottom of the slope and build in layers. Choose the best-looking stone to start building your rockery and position it in the middle so that the strata lines angle gently back into the ground. About one-third of the stone will be underground, so you will have to scoop out a hole to accommodate it. Then add stones either side so that the strata lines

HOW TO PLANT A ROCK GARDEN

1 Position the plants while still in their pots so that you can see how they look and adjust if necessary. Alpines are a good choice of plant for a rock garden.

2 Use a trowel to take out a hole a little larger than the rootball. You can buy narrow trowels that are particularly useful for planting in the crevices between rocks.

3 Make sure that the plant is at the correct depth, then trickle gritty soil around the roots and firm it well.

4 Finish off by covering the exposed surface with more grit to improve drainage and protect leaves from splashing mud.

fall away at exactly the same angle. Make sure that each stone is set firm before positioning the next by ramming soil around the rock. Repeat the process for each layer of the rockery, then fill any gaps with a

free-draining mixture consisting of equal parts of good quality topsoil, peat (or peat substitute) and coarse grit. Then plant and mulch the surface with stone chippings to match the rocks used in the rockery.

4 Lever the next row of rocks into position. Using rollers and levers is the best way to move heavy rocks around.

5 As each layer is built up, add more of the soil mixture and consolidate it around each of the rocks in turn.

6 Make sure that the sides slope inwards and make the top reasonably flat rather than building it into a pinnacle. Position the plants, then cover the exposed soil with a layer of stone chippings.

Basic techniques

There are a range of basic gardening techniques, such as weeding, watering and feeding, that are common to most if not all parts of the garden. They are all easy to understand and take little skill to master, so it is worth spending some time getting these techniques right because they can have a considerable impact on the rest of your gardening.

Carrying out simple tasks correctly can often save you hours of time later. Weeding, for example, is best carried out before you plant up a bed. Once the flowers and shrubs have been planted and a thick layer of mulch added, the bed will need very little weeding.

Once the basic tasks have been mastered, you will have the time to carry out more elaborate and challenging techniques. Do remember to take sensible safety precautions to prevent injury and ensure gardening remains a pleasure.

As well as being the ideal place to store your tools, equipment and other gardening materials, a shed can be an attractive retreat in its own dusty way.

Essential tool kit

You don't need a shed full of tools to be able to garden successfully, but you will find some items indispensable and can build up your kit as you go.

Choosing tools

If tools are going to be used they need to be effective, convenient and comfortable to use, and it is always worth trying out new tools before making your selection. Always buy the best you can afford, because well-made and well-maintained garden tools will last a lifetime.

Tools for digging You will need some form of digging tool, such as a spade or fork. A spade is perhaps the more versatile but a fork is better on stony ground or if you find digging particularly hard work. Smaller, easy-to-use border forks are also available. Whatever digging tool you select, choose a make that is strong, with a comfortable handle that is long enough to prevent you stooping when you dig; long-handled versions are available to suit taller gardeners. Make sure

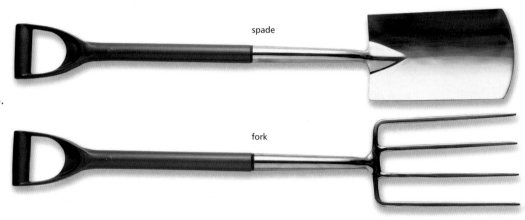
spade

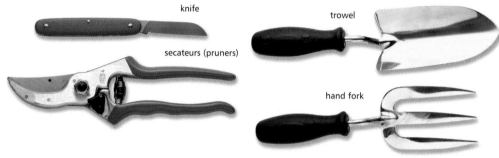
fork

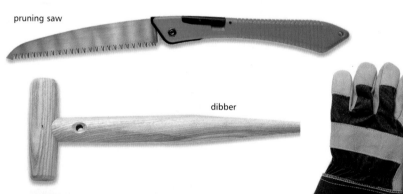
knife

trowel

secateurs (pruners)

hand fork

pruning saw

gloves

dibber

Rosa 'Zéphirine Drouhin', *Clematis* 'Lady Betty Balfour' and *Vitis coignetiae* need regular pruning to keep them in good shape. Use secateurs (pruners) or long-handled loppers to cut them back.

Lawn care equipment

If you have a lawn you will need a range of specialist equipment, including a mower with a cutting width to suit the size of your lawn, a pair of shears or a nylon-line trimmer to keep the edges in trim and a spring-tined (wire or lawn) rake with springy, wire-like tines set at an angle for combing through grass to remove dead leaves, moss and thatch.

the grip of a D-shaped handle is wide enough to be comfortable when you are wearing gloves. Stainless steel tools are more expensive but might be worth the investment if your soil is particularly heavy. If you intend to do a lot of digging choose tools with a tread (a flat area on top of the blade to put your foot on) because this will be more comfortable and be less damaging to your footwear.

Tools for weeding Most gardeners will find a hoe of some kind invaluable. The style you choose is a personal matter, but Dutch and draw hoes have stood the test of time. Again, choose one with a handle that is long enough for your height and make sure the head is securely fastened to the shaft. The Dutch hoe is the easier to master and more versatile, using a simple push and pull action to chop off weeds just below the soil surface. The shape of a draw hoe makes it easier to draw up soil around plants and to use among plants in existing borders.

Tools for levelling soil There are several types of rake, each designed for very specific purposes, but for most gardeners a soil rake is most frequently used. It usually has about a dozen, equally spaced, solid metal, vertical teeth and is used for levelling soil and removing stones before planting or sowing.

Tools for cutting These are also an essential element in the basic gardening tool kit. A well-made, straight-bladed, all-purpose knife is top of the list because it has a multitude of uses around the garden. A sturdy pair of secateurs (pruners) for deadheading and most types of pruning is also essential, but if serious pruning is contemplated, a pair of long-handled loppers or a pruning saw will be needed, too.

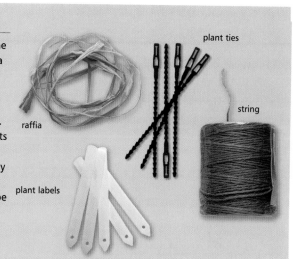

Labelling and tying

When you are working in the garden, it is useful to have a tray of odds and ends, such as string, raffia, plant ties and labels. You never know when you might need them. For example, wayward shoots of climbers may need fixing to their supports, or you may be sowing seeds or planting seedlings that you need to be able to identify.

raffia

plant ties

string

plant labels

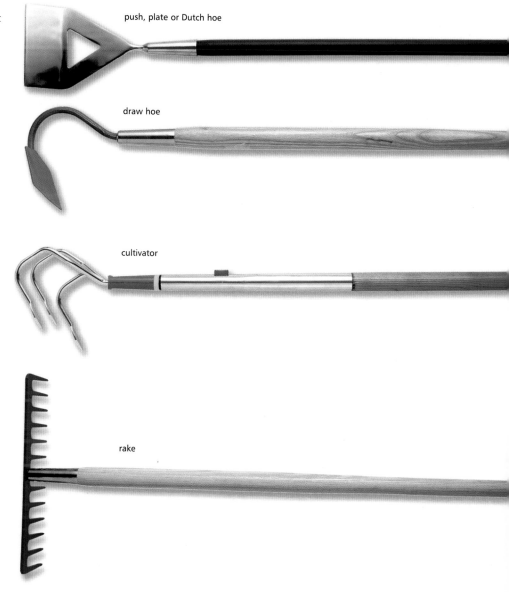

push, plate or Dutch hoe

draw hoe

cultivator

rake

Weeding

Weeds are nothing more than plants growing where they are not wanted. There are several techniques you can adopt to reduce the number of weeds in the garden and, therefore, the time spent weeding.

Controlling weeds

There are two types of weeds: annual weeds, such as groundsel and chickweed, which grow from seed, flower and set seed again in one season; and perennial weeds, such as dock, bindweed, couch grass and thistle, which survive for more than two growing seasons and often many years. It is important to remove all weeds before they flower and set seed, otherwise you will be weeding for many seasons to come – after all, a single weed can scatter many thousands of viable seeds near and far.

Weeds will be able to grow only if there is bare soil waiting for them to colonize, so you can go a long way to preventing weeds by covering all the bare soil in your garden: by planting up your borders and filling any gaps with ground cover plants or mulches. Alternatively, you can use a special chemical between established woody plants, such as trees and shrubs, to inhibit the germination of weed seeds. Such products will also damage the new growth of desirable plants, so they are not suitable for mixed borders containing herbaceous perennials or bulbs.

The best way to tackle weeds depends both on the type of weeds you have and where they are growing. In general, annual weeds are easy to control by using a hoe in open spaces between plants and by hand to remove weeds among ornamental plants. Perennial weeds are more difficult to eliminate because you have to remove the entire root as well as the topgrowth, otherwise the weed is likely to re-sprout. This can be hard work with some weeds, such

HOW TO WEED

1 Deep-rooted perennial weeds that have long, penetrating roots are best forked up. Loosen the roots with a fork, and hold the stem close to its base as you pull up the whole plant. If you don't get all the root out, the plant may re-grow.

2 Hoeing is one of the best forms of annual weed control, but it needs to be done fairly regularly. Slice the weeds off just beneath the soil, preferably when the soil is dry. Keep beds and borders as well as the vegetable garden hoed throughout the growing season.

3 Contact chemical weedkillers are useful if you need to clear an area of ground quickly and easily. Some types, which normally kill only the top growth so are better for annuals than problem perennial weeds, leave the area safe to replant after a day.

4 Systematic weedkillers kill the whole plant. Large areas can be sprayed, but some formulations can be painted on the leaves so will not harm other plants. Some types break down immediately in the soil.

5 Mulches are an effective method of controlling weeds. In the vegetable and fruit garden various forms of matting and plastic sheeting are a cost-effective method.

6 Where appearance matters, use a mulch of an organic material, such as chipped bark or garden compost. If the ground is cleared first a mulch at least 5cm (2in) – ideally 8cm (3in) – thick will suppress most weeds.

USING CHEMICAL WEEDKILLERS

A chemical weedkiller is best used to kill persistent weeds when first preparing a bed. Avoid using chemicals near fruit, vegetables or herbs. Always follow the manufacturer's instructions on the packet.

as dandelions and thistles, which produce a carrot-like taproot, and for brittle-rooted weeds, such as couch grass and bindweed, which send out roots in all directions, it can be close to impossible. Indeed, if these weeds have become established in your garden, you may have to dig up the entire border and painstakingly remove every weed root you can find before replanting the ornamental plants. If this is not a practical option you could try exhausting the weeds into submission by removing all the topgrowth and repeating the process every time it re-sprouts.

Your final option is to use a chemical weedkiller, which should be applied according to the instructions on the pack. There are two main types: contact weedkillers, which kill the parts of the weed they touch; and systemic formulations, which are transported around the plant, killing all parts. Which you choose will depend on personal preference and where the weeds are growing.

Beds and borders

Hand-weed mixed borders and use a hoe to clear annual weeds from bare soil between plants. Perennial weeds can be removed by hand where practicable or killed with a spot treatment weedkiller. Large weeds are easier to treat with a glyphosate-based, ready-to-use spray, but cover all nearby ornamental plants with a plastic sheet before spraying and leave the sheet in position until the spray is dry.

Lawns

Remove isolated weeds by hand using an old knife or a special weeding tool. Alternatively, kill them using a spot weedkiller. If the weed problem is more widespread, it is more efficient to use a specially formulated lawn weedkiller.

Where moss is also a problem it is a good idea to use a combined moss and weedkiller treatment in spring.

Patios and paths

Remove individual weeds by hand using an old knife or a special weeding tool. Alternatively, kill them with a spot weedkiller. Where the problem is widespread use a path weedkiller, which will kill existing weeds and prevent further weed problems for the rest of the year.

Neglected areas

If there are no ornamental plants, dig over the entire area, hand-weeding as you go. If this is not practicable, remove all the topgrowth and cover the area with black plastic or old carpet for a few years. A glyphosate-based weedkiller is another option. Stubborn weeds, such as bramble, may need several applications, or you could use the more potent chemical, sodium chlorate, although you will not be able to plant the treated area for at least six weeks afterwards.

The close planting of vigorous perennials, such as *Dictamnus albus* (dittany), prevents weed seedlings from germinating and surviving.

Ground cover

Weeding is a time-consuming task, and it is best to prevent weeds from germinating in the first place if you can. Carpeting the ground with a mass of attractive foliage, which also makes an effective foil for other plants and may produce flowers itself, makes good gardening sense.

What is a ground cover plant?

To make a suitable ground covering, a plant needs to establish quickly and cover the ground with a dense layer of leaves, without any gaps where weeds could germinate. The principle is that the plant is so dense that little light can reach the ground and any weed seedlings that do manage to germinate are starved of light, become sickly, and soon die.

The ground cover plant should also be low growing, so as not to detract from the ornamental plants,

The dense ground cover subshrub *Lithodora diffusa* makes a vivid carpet of blue in spring.

and not so invasive that it swamps the whole bed. Although a wide variety of plants are labelled and described as suitable, relatively few make ideal ground cover.

Choosing the right ground cover

Low-growing ground cover plants are an ideal way of covering the soil between shrubs and trees in the border. Choose plants that are ground-hugging and can cope with the occasional trampling; you will need to tread on them to carry out maintenance to other plants.

Try to select plants with foliage that will contrast with the other plants, so that they set one another off. An underplanting of bulbs will provide seasonal variation and interest: tulips, spring-flowering dwarf narcissi and autumn-flowering colchicums are suitable. Some plants, such as heather or *Hypericum calycinum*, also have flowers to enhance their appearance.

Ground cover is also useful for areas where grass is not practical. For example, *Hypericum calycinum* is useful on slopes that are difficult to mow,

while *Vinca minor* is good for awkward areas at the bottom of a fence or alongside a driveway. Ground cover plants also make a low-maintenance option in the front garden.

A few ground cover plants, such as cotoneaster and prostrate junipers, produce stiff spreading foliage, which lends itself to covering eyesores such as manhole covers or ugly tree stumps.

Planting and aftercare

Although ground cover will prevent weeds from establishing, they do need to be planted into weed-free ground to start with. The best time to plant is autumn.

Prepare the ground by digging thoroughly and removing weeds, including the roots of perennial weeds. Incorporate well-rotted manure and a handful of bonemeal per square metre (yard). Take care not to damage the roots of existing plants if you are planting between or under them. When planting ground cover, do so either through a mulch matting or mulch after planting with an 8cm (3in) thick layer of loose

DIVIDING GROUND COVER

If you buy large ground cover plants in containers, they can be divided before planting for maximum cover. Gently knock the plant, such as this *Pachysandra terminalis*, out of its pot without damaging the roots. If the crown is too tough to pull or prise apart, try cutting through it with a knife. Replant larger pieces with several shoots and plenty of roots immediately. Smaller pieces can be potted up and grown on for a year before planting out into the garden. Keep new plants well watered until they are established.

HOW TO PLANT GROUND COVER

1 Clear the ground of weeds first, and be especially careful to remove any deep-rooted or persistent perennial weeds.

2 Add plenty of garden compost or rotted manure, then rake in a slow-release fertilizer or bonemeal. This will help the plants establish successfully.

3 Cover the area with a weed-suppressing mulching sheet. The special semi-permeable membrane allows water and air to penetrate to the soil.

4 Make crossed slits through the mulching sheet where you want to plant. Avoid making the slits too large.

5 Excavate holes and plant the ground cover, firming in well. If necessary, tease a few of the roots apart first.

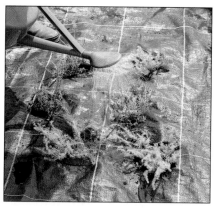

6 Water thoroughly, and keep well watered. In prominent positions you could disguise the mulching sheet with a thin layer of soil.

organic mulch to prevent weeds from germinating before the ground cover can do the job. The distance between each of the ground cover plants will depend on the vigour of the plant you have chosen and how long you are prepared to wait for complete cover. Obviously, the closer the spacing the more plants you will need and the costlier it will be.

Good ground cover plants should remain pest and disease free and require little maintenance, other than an annual tidy up. This is best done in late autumn when deciduous leaves that have become trapped in the stems can be collected.

Good ground cover plants

Shrubs
Berberis thunbergii 'Atropurpurea Nana'
Calluna vulgaris cultivars
Ceanothus thyrsiflorus var. repens
Cotoneaster dammeri
Cotoneaster x suecicus 'Coral Beauty'
Erica carnea cultivars
Euonymus fortunei 'Emerald Gaiety'
Gaultheria procumbens
Genista lydia
Hebe pinguifolia 'Pagei'
Hypericum calycinum
Juniperus horizontalis Glauca Group
Juniperus squamata 'Blue Carpet'
Mahonia aquifolium
Vinca minor

Perennials
Ajuga reptans
Alchemilla mollis (lady's mantle)
Bergenia (elephant's ears)
Convallaria majalis (lily-of-the-valley)
Epimedium perralderianum
Geranium
Heuchera
Hosta sieboldiana
Houttuynia cordata
Lamium maculatum
Lysimachia nummularia (creeping Jenny)
Nepeta 'Six Hills Giant'
Pulmonaria (lungwort)
Rodgersia
Symphytum (comfrey)

Mulching

A mulch is a layer of material laid on the soil surface to discourage weeds from germinating and to prevent moisture loss. Organic mulches also improve soil fertility.

Types of mulch

The most natural mulch is loose organic material laid over the surface of the soil in a layer 8cm (3in) deep. In nature autumn leaves provide a blanket of organic matter, but in the garden we can use anything from chipped bark or cocoa shells to garden compost, leafmould or grass clippings. Non-organic mulches are used too, such as stone chippings and pebbles, or manufactured sheet mulches, as well as old carpet and black polythene.

A mulch helps to retain moisture in the soil by preventing water evaporating from the surface layer. Dark coloured mulches can also help warm the soil early in the season and promote rapid root growth in spring.

Organic mulches

These are popular because they are easy to use, adaptable and help to improve soil fertility as they slowly decompose and are incorporated into the soil by earthworms and other soil-dwelling creatures. Some, such as bark chippings, composted bark and cocoa shells, are attractive to look at and provide a useful foil for low-growing border plants and bulbs. Bear in mind that loose organic mulches, such as grass clippings, that have not been composted will deplete the levels of nitrogen in the soil surface as they decompose. They are suitable for use only between established plants or alongside a hedge.

Inorganic mulches

Loose inorganic mulches are particularly useful in certain areas of the garden. Pea gravel, for example, is ideal around alpines, which like well-drained conditions and would rot if surrounded with a loose

organic mulch. Similarly, stone chippings are often the best choice for covering the soil in planting pockets and between paving slabs in and around the patio. Pebbles, on the other hand, are ideal for mulching around plants, such as clematis, which like to have a cool root run, or as an attractive finishing touch to containers.

If you are planting a new bed or a specimen tree or shrub, specially made sheet mulches are an option worth considering. This material, also called mulch matting, is permeable and weed-proof. Lay the sheet over the prepared soil before

DIFFERENT TYPES OF MULCH

A border without any kind of mulch on the soil is prone to weed infestation and to loss of moisture.

Grass cuttings are readily available in most gardens. They are not attractive but can be used effectively between established plants at the back of borders, where they are not highly visible. Do not heap them on thicker than 5cm (2in) or they may heat up too much as they decompose, harming the plant.

Composted bark is an ideal material for mulching, being both effective and attractive. Do not use bark that is fresh, however, or the resin may harm the plants. Hedge and shrub prunings can be shredded and used after they have been composted for a couple of months.

This bright border has been well tended, resulting in the vigorous growth of healthy plants. An organic mulch of well-rotted garden compost was applied early in spring to return nutrients to the soil and to prevent weed seeds from germinating.

planting up a bed and simply cut cross-shaped slits in the sheet at each planting position. For larger plants, place a sheet over the soil around the specimen after planting, covering an area of at least 1sq m (1sq yard) around each plant. Sheet mulches are more effective weed barriers than loose organic mulches and do not need to be reapplied every spring. They do not, however, improve soil fertility and are unattractive. They are best disguised with a thin layer of soil or a mulch if used in prominent positions.

Semi-permeable mulching membrane, which has small holes in it to allow water and air to pass through to the soil, is available from many garden retailers. Measure out how much you will need, then cut the membrane to shape and lay it on the surface of the soil.

Mulching membrane is fairly unattractive so, in prominent positions, it is worth disguising it with a layer of gravel to improve the appearance of the border. Make sure that the membrane is flat and completely covered with stones.

Material mulches are not suitable to cover areas planted with bulbs or dormant herbaceous plants. In such positions, a loose organic or inorganic mulch such as gravel would be a better option.

Watering and feeding

Watering and feeding are among the most time-consuming tasks in the garden, especially if you have a lot of containers or own a greenhouse. Use the following techniques to help you work efficiently.

Watering

The ground must be thoroughly soaked after watering: a sprinkling will do little other than lay the dust. Effective watering should supply the equivalent of 2.5cm (1in) of rain.

Every gardener should have a watering can fitted with a fine rose, and this may be all that you need if your garden is small or if you do not grow many plants in containers. Most gardeners, however, will benefit from installing an outside tap (faucet) fitted with a hose on a reel. This will make transporting water around the garden straightforward, and the reel will keep your hose neat and tidy.

Ideally, the hose should be long enough to reach all parts of the garden, but if this is not possible it should certainly reach the areas that require the most frequent watering, such as the patio, greenhouse and kitchen garden. An adjustable nozzle at the end of the hose is a good idea as this will eliminate the need to keep returning to the tap to regulate the supply. If you have a lot of hanging baskets, window boxes or other out-of-the-way containers a hose lance (hose wand) that directs the water is a good investment.

A hose-end sprinkler is worth considering for large areas. Choose an oscillating or rotary type for the most even coverage. However, most garden plants do not need regular watering, even during a drought, and because the water is applied indiscriminately over the entire area a great deal is wasted. It is, moreover, tempting to leave the tap running for longer than is really necessary.

If you cannot afford the time to water all your plants on a regular basis, you can buy systems that will do the job for you. For most gardeners, the best option is a system of micro-bore tubes that carry water to individual plants. These networks usually have an adjustable nozzle fitted to regulate the correct amount of water. Such systems can be used for watering all types of container, including hanging baskets, and can also be linked to lengths of leaky pipe (sometimes called a seep hose or drip hose) for watering plants in

WATERING SYSTEMS

Most automatic watering systems have a control system to reduce the water pressure, and some act as a filter to prevent nozzles becoming clogged.

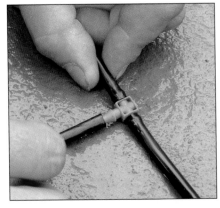

Drip-feed systems can be used for beds, borders and containers. T-joints allow tubes to be attached for individual drip heads.

The delivery nozzle of this drip-feed system is held in position with a pipe peg, so that the head can deliver water to an individual plant.

A seep or drip hose can be laid along a row of plants and will water only the immediate area. The water slowly seeps out of the pipe and soaks into the soil.

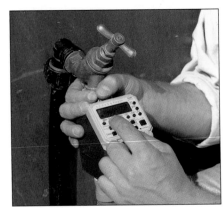

A timing device will turn water on and off automatically. You can preset the timing, so this is an ideal way of watering your plants while you are away on holiday.

HOW TO APPLY FERTILIZER

If it is necessary to pep up a flagging border towards the end of a long season, add a liquid feed to a watering can. Follow the instructions given by the manufacturer.

If you want to apply a foliar feed to a large number of plants, use a special applicator fitted to the end of a garden hose so that a measured amount is applied.

Dry fertilizer can simply be scattered on the soil around individual plants that need feeding, so there is no waste.

rows, such as in fruit and vegetable gardens. Plumbing the system to an outside tap (faucet) and including a water timer or watering computer will give a completely automatic watering system.

Collecting your own water

Place a water butt beneath the gutter of a greenhouse, shed or garage to catch the water as it runs off the roof. Rain water is slightly acidic so ideal for watering acid-loving plants, especially if you live in a hard-water area. It will also save water and money spent on metered water.

You can easily collect sufficient water in a water butt to keep a collection of acid-loving plants happy all summer long. If you are more ambitious you can now get kits to link water butts together to create a serious garden water storage system.

The butt should be easy to use, so make sure there is room to get a watering can under the tap. Keep the butt covered at all times so that the water remains sweet and clean.

You can also recycle water that has been used for washing or bathing in the house. Known as "grey-water", it is suitable for applying to established plants in borders and on lawns, but is best used immediately not stored.

Feeding

The other regular task facing the gardener during the summer is feeding. Plants in containers will quickly deplete the fertilizer present in the potting compost (soil mix)

unless a slow-release fertilizer was added at the planting time. You will need to feed weekly from about six weeks after planting.

Some fertilizers are formulated for specific plants – tomatoes, roses and lawn grass are the best known – but most gardeners will also find a general fertilizer of some kind useful. These fertilizers are supplied in powder or liquid form and may need to be diluted or made up according to the manufacturer's recommendations. Alternatively, you can add a slow-release fertilizer to the compost in the form of pellets or granules. These will usually provide sufficient nutrients for a growing season.

When planting permanent borders of trees and shrubs, add a slow-release fertilizer, such as bonemeal, and improve the soil with well-rotted organic matter.

In a very small garden or in the greenhouse, a watering can is probably the most efficient way to deliver the appropriate amount of your chosen feed to individual plants. In a large garden a special attachment for a garden hose can be used to deliver fertilizer over a large area.

Pests and diseases

The best way to control pests and diseases is to maintain a healthy garden environment and grow plants well so that they are able to shrug off or recover quickly from most attacks. It is also worth seeking out problem-free varieties that are naturally resistant to attack.

Deterring pests and diseases

Good garden hygiene is the most important factor in the battle against pests and diseases. Clear all debris from around the garden and put suitable material on the compost heap. Consign the rest to the dustbin or bonfire as soon as you can. Clean containers once you finish using them. Stay vigilant for the first signs of attack and take necessary remedial action as soon as possible. Keep weeds under control, including during the winter, because they can provide a convenient overwintering site for some problems.

Nectar-rich plants

Shrubs and trees	Iberis
Buddleia	*Limnanthes*
Crataegus	*Lunaria*
Viburnum	*Matthiola*
	Sedum
Flowers	*Solidago*
Arabis	
Aubrieta	
Erysimum	

Encouraging natural predators

A well-managed garden will be a dangerous place for pests because it is full of natural predators including birds, small mammals, amphibians, spiders and insects. You can increase the numbers of these natural predators by providing them with food, shelter and suitable places to breed. Frogs and toads, for example, are voracious eaters of slugs and will happily take up residence if you provide suitable places for them to

Natural predators

Introducing or encouraging beneficial insects can have a dramatic impact on the number of pests in your garden. Check which pests your plants are vulnerable to, and encourage their natural predators into your garden.

Ladybirds (ladybugs) and larvae – eat aphids, scale insects, mealy bugs and caterpillars

Hoverflies and larvae – eat up to 50 aphids a day

Lacewings – eat aphids, woolly aphids, spider mites, scale insects and caterpillars

Ground beetles – eat slugs, flat worms, cabbage and carrot rootfly (eggs and larvae), vine weevils and spider mites

Anthocorid bugs – eat vine weevil larvae, caterpillars, midge larvae and spider mites

Centipedes – eat slugs and snails

PREVENTING DISEASE

Thoroughly wash and clean pots, trays and equipment after use to get rid of loose soil that may harbour pests and diseases.

There are many beautiful garden plants that have the added advantage of attracting the natural predators of pests into the garden. This wallflower (*Erysimum*) is nectar-rich and will attract bees and butterflies, as well as hoverflies and lacewings.

WEEDING

Continue to weed vegetable and flower beds during the winter. Weeds can harbour pests and diseases that will attack plants later.

HOW TO TREAT MILDEW

1 Mildew is common in humid conditions, so apply a mulch to keep the roots moist but do not water the leaves.

2 Remove leaves affected by mildew. Severely damaged plants can be sprayed with a suitable fungicide.

hide and a pond where they can breed. Similarly, useful insects, such as hoverflies, can be lured into your garden by nectar-rich plants and a supply of insect pests. You can even provide a "hotel", made from bundles of bamboo, where they can safely hibernate.

Controlling pests and diseases
Stay one step ahead of the pests by sowing and planting at appropriate times and putting up traps and barriers. Protecting plants with suitable netting is probably the only solution to prevent damage caused by mammals such as rabbits. Isolated

attacks of snails and caterpillars can be picked off by hand and destroyed, while small colonies of aphids can be rubbed out between finger and thumb. Similarly, isolated disease symptoms can be pruned out and the affected material put in the dustbin or burned. Do not put any material that looks as if it has been attacked by disease in the compost bin, as this may spread the disease to other plants in the garden.

It is worth having a few chemicals to hand for the most intransigent pests and diseases. Slug pellets, for example, can be used sparingly around vulnerable plants, notably

hostas, when they are planted out, and each spring thereafter, before the new leaves emerge.

If you have problems with aphids, choose a selective treatment based on pirimicarb, which is specific to aphids. A systemic insecticide is also useful for all other insect pests. Choose one based on permethrin or dimethoate or a spray based on pyrethrum if you garden organically.

Combined chemical treatments can be very quick and effective. Many rose growers, for example, like to use a combined treatment to combat the three main rose diseases of blackspot, mildew and rust.

HOW TO DEAL WITH CATERPILLARS AND SLUGS

The best way to get rid of caterpillars, such as these on *Polygonatum odoratum*, is to pick them off by hand.

When slugs and snails eat holes in hosta leaves, the holes remain visible throughout the growing season. If you do not mind using slug pellets, scatter them around the plants.

Dishes and jars half-filled with beer or sweetened water and sunk into the ground will attract slugs and snails, which can be collected up and disposed of.

Safety in the garden

The garden can be a dangerous place if you are careless. Every year thousands of people are injured by garden equipment, particularly power tools. Fortunately, most of the injuries are avoidable if you take the necessary precautions when using the equipment.

Think ahead

Always take sensible steps to protect yourself when gardening. Wear thick gloves when handling rough materials and protect your eyes with goggles when pruning or working with twiggy stems.

Pruning

Move around a plant to prune it rather than stretching to your furthest reach. Use a steady ladder if you are cutting a hedge or climber over shoulder height.

Most accidents that involve a hedgetrimmer occur when the machine is in use, with lacerations, falls and electrocutions (with electric

Thorny plants, such as this rose 'Ispahan', should be pruned back from a path or a doorway to prevent the stems catching on passers-by.

models) coming top of the list. Make sure your machine has the basic safety features such as a short blade-stopping time, two-handed switches and special blade extensions that stick out beyond the reciprocating blades and prevent you cutting something accidentally.

Always use the appropriate clothing and a thick pair of gloves. Use a hedgetrimmer with care and don't try to rush the job. Keep both hands on the machine while it is in operation.

Lawnmowers

Most lawnmower accidents, on the other hand, occur when the machine is not being used. Be particularly careful while it is being cleaned, maintained or simply moved around. Check that the blade has stopped moving before removing the box, and disengage the machine from the power supply before touching the blade. Turn off the power supply to electric models and turn off the engine and disconnect the spark plug lead with petrol-driven machines. If the blades become clogged, use a stick to clear them.

Of the accidents that occur while a mower is being used, most are because the machine is being asked to do too much — either the grass is overgrown, wet or both — or is on a steep incline. If you have a steeply sloping lawn always mow across the slope rather than up and down it.

HOW TO PRUNE SAFELY

1 It is sensible to use a hedgetrimmer on a large or fast-growing hedge, but power tools such as this can be dangerous. Accidents often occur when you are in a hurry, so take your time and don't start pruning unless you know you can finish the job comfortably.

2 Pruning very tall climbers is a job that requires some care. Check that the feet of the ladder are steady on the ground. Do not attempt to reach too far above your head or stretch to the left or right. It is better to move the ladder than risk overbalancing.

Shredders

Most accidents occur either when the blades are being unblocked, or when the equipment is being used without the correct safety guards in place. Always wear eye protection and strong gloves. If you are using a shredder for a long period of time, wear ear defenders too. Never put your hand in inlets or outlets and only try to shred materials recommended by the manufacturer.

Using chemicals

If you are dealing with chemicals make sure you follow all of the manufacturer's instructions, including using protective equipment or clothing, such as waterproof gloves when handling concentrates, and washing your hands and the equipment thoroughly after spraying. Do not apply at rates not given on the packet or make chemical cocktails unless it is specifically advised in the instructions. Only apply chemicals when the prevailing weather conditions are suitable and make sure spray does not drift on to other areas of the garden. Always dispose of chemicals as directed.

ADDING BONEMEAL

It is advisable to wear protective gloves when you are adding bonemeal to the soil as there is a small risk of it harbouring disease.

USING POWER TOOLS

Always read the safety instructions supplied by the manufacturer carefully before using power tools, and follow them to the letter.

Essential tool maintenance

Having invested in a set of good quality gardening tools it makes sense to keep them in good condition. Not only will they last longer, but they will be easier and more efficient to use. Always keep bladed tools sharp so that they cut efficiently, causing as little damage to the plant tissue as possible – particularly important when pruning and propagating. It also makes sense to keep the blades of spades and hoes sharp. When storing tools make sure that all bare metal parts are clean, and have an oily rag to hand so that they can be lightly oiled before being put away. Larger tools such as border forks and spades that don't have a really sharp edge can be stood in an old bucket of oily sand when they are not needed.

Most garden cutting equipment does not require routine maintenance, other than cleaning and replacing worn blades. If you do intend to use a service centre, to service a petrol machine for example, do it at the end of the season rather than waiting until the centres are busy in the spring, when frustrating delays inevitably occur.

Seasonal checklist

Many of the basic maintenance tasks required in the garden are seasonal: they depend either on a particular stage of growth or on environmental conditions to be effective. For example, it is important to choose the right time of year to prune roses, otherwise you risk losing a year's worth of flowers. It is, therefore, important to know the optimum time for each technique.

The following pages summarize the main tasks you are most likely to need throughout the year. These tasks are divided into the gardening seasons of spring; early summer; late summer; and autumn and winter, rather than the seasons of the year. The techniques are listed according to the areas of the garden they apply to. Use them as a quick guide to your gardening activities but remember that nothing in gardening is prescriptive, and the timing will depend on your garden, the weather and the time you have available.

Many gardeners enjoy the routine maintenance tasks needed throughout the year. Early preparation can pay dividends later.

Spring techniques

For many gardeners, spring is the most exciting time of the year. This is when plants begin to show signs of new life and the garden is full of promise. It isn't long before the first spring flowers make their spectacular appearance.

Beds and borders

Prune shrubs Prune early-flowering shrubs, such as forsythia, as soon as flowering is over. Prune grey-leaved shrubs, such as lavenders, to keep them compact and bushy.

Apply fertilizer After pruning shrubs apply a slow-release fertilizer on the ground during mid-spring to give them a boost.

Feed and mulch Add a good layer of organic matter to beds and borders. This will not only feed the soil, but will also prevent weeds from growing and help the soil to retain moisture.

Slugs and snails Protect emerging shoots of vulnerable plants, such as hostas, from the attention of slugs and snails.

Deadhead bulbs Remove fading blooms from bulbs but leave the foliage intact for at least a further six weeks.

Bluebells will naturalize in shady areas, providing a sweetly scented carpet in late spring.

Start weeding Remove weeds from beds and borders before they are able to flower and set seed.

Compost heap As soon as the weather warms up, turn the compost heap in order to ensure even composting.

Check equipment Make sure all garden tools and machinery are in good working order before you will be using them in earnest. It is important to check that cutting tools are sharp and electrical equipment is safe, including cables and connectors.

New plants Mid-spring is an ideal time to plant all types of hardy plants, including deciduous and evergreen trees, shrubs and climbers and hardy herbaceous plants. Wait until late spring to plant conifers. Buy bulbs and seed in mid-spring.

Planting out Sow sweet peas in early spring and plant out in mid-spring.

Tidy up The rock garden can be tidied up now. Apply a fresh layer of stone chippings where necessary.

Harden off Tender bedding plants should be hardened off in late spring.

Lawns

First cut When the grass is dry, give the lawn its first cut. Set the cutting height of the mower to 2.5cm (1in). After a few weeks, reduce the cutting height to 2cm (¾in) for most lawns, or to 1.5cm (½in) for a fine finish. Regularly mow the lawn from mid-spring onwards.

New lawns Mid- to late spring is an ideal time to create a new lawn.

APPLY FERTILIZER

Apply a slow-release fertilizer around shrubs to give them an added boost.

DEADHEAD BULBS

Remove the flowerheads of daffodils before the seed has time to develop.

Prepare the ground thoroughly as soon as weather conditions allow and either sow seed or lay turf.

Control moss Apply a moss killer in mid-spring when the grass is dry if your lawn has been colonized by moss over winter. Use a wire rake to remove the moss at least a fortnight after applying the chemical control. If you need to give your lawn a boost, too, use a combined moss killer and lawn fertilizer treatment.

Make repairs Remove any large weeds using an old kitchen knife and control coarse grasses by either digging them out or weakening them by slashing them with a knife each time you mow. Any bare patches can be reseeded in mid-spring.

Ponds

Position pump If an electric heater has been kept in the pool for winter, it can be removed now and the filter started up if it was turned off for the winter. Replace the pond pump in mid-spring.

Cutting back Any brown stems left on marginal and moisture-loving plants for winter attraction or protection for shy creatures can be cut back. Ornamental grasses should be pruned to just above the new green shoots.

Feed fish Start feeding fish in the pond in mid-spring, as soon as they become active.

Protecting fish Herons are at their hungriest in spring, so take the necessary precautions to protect fish.

Plant up On a warm day in late spring or early summer plant up your pond or add new plants to an existing feature. Replace tender plants that have been overwintered in a frost-free place.

Keeping the pond area clean Clean off algae from paved or wooden surfaces around the pond.

USE CLOCHES

Particularly tender plants should be protected with glass or plastic cloches until all threat of frost has passed.

Plant protection Protect sensitive plants by placing horticultural fleece over the flowers if late frosts are forecast. The young growth of plants, such as giant rhubarb (*Gunnera manicata*), should have a protective covering of dead leaves until all danger of frosts has passed.

Lifting plants The young growth of tender marginals such as mimulus and lobelia, which has been protected by thick organic mulches, will be sprouting. Lift the plants and divide

FEED FISH

Floating pelleted food allows you to see if the fish are using up the food quickly. Start feeding fish in mid-spring.

them or take cuttings of the young shoots and root them in a frost-free greenhouse.

Look out for algal growth Spring sunshine could spark off algal growth in shallow pools where the surface is clear until the waterlily leaves begin to grow. This should correct itself as the leaves develop.

Cut back The shoots of coppiced waterside shrubs, such as dogwoods and the coloured-stemmed willow, should be cut back.

Pale yellow primroses, tiny forget-me-nots and the delicate flowers of dicentras make a lovely fresh combination for a spring border.

Early summer techniques

This is the busiest time of the gardener's year, with plenty to do in every part of the garden. Seedlings and established plants will need constant attention. Early summer is also a transitional period, and there is often an interval between the spring flowering plants dying back and the peak of colour offered by abundant summer bedding.

Beds and borders

Position supports Place supports around tall herbaceous plants during late spring or early summer to prevent them flopping over when in full bloom. Stake single-stemmed plants, such as delphiniums and gladioli, with canes.

Plant containers Plant up hanging baskets and summer containers with bedding plants and place outside after the threat of frost has passed.

Feed container plants About a month after planting up containers (including growing bags) start to feed with liquid feed unless you added a slow-release fertilizer at planting time. Use a balanced feed on beds and borders

The hardy geraniums are one of the mainstays of the summer border. There is a wide range from which to choose.

PRUNE CLIMBERS

Early flowering clematis (Group 1) should be pruned after blooming.

and a high-potash fertilizer, such as tomato feed, for flowering and fruiting plants.

Deadhead flowers Remove faded blooms from repeat-flowering plants such as roses. Annual bedding should also be deadheaded where practical to encourage further flushes of blooms. Deadhead self-seeders, such as forget-me-nots (*Myosotis*) and campanulas, to prevent them becoming a weed problem. Once flowering has finished, deadhead rhododendrons, taking care not to damage or remove the buds for next year that lie just below this year's blooms.

Pest watch Stay vigilant for the first signs of pests and disease attacks, especially aphids, which can attack plants all around the garden; take appropriate action promptly. Spray susceptible roses against blackspot, mildew and rust. Hand-pick any caterpillars and sawfly grubs.

Slugs and snails Continue to protect emerging shoots of vulnerable plants such as hostas against attacks from slugs and snails.

Water new plants Make sure new plants do not run short of water during their first growing season. Mulch after watering to help retain soil moisture and minimize competition from weeds. Also water container plants as necessary.

Prune shrubs Prune early summer-flowering shrubs, such as choisya, deutzia, kerria, lilac, philadelphus, spiraea and tamarix, as soon as the flowering is over.

Tie in climbers New growth produced by climbers should be tied into the support to keep the plant looking tidy and to avoid damage to the shoots. The stems will still be easy to manoeuvre in early summer.

Keep weeding Continue to remove weeds as they appear.

Lawns

Keep mowing Mow the lawn regularly as necessary, generally at least once a week but twice a week if the grass is growing strongly. During dry spells, growth will slow and the need for mowing will be reduced; also raise the cutting height of your mower.

Watering lawns Water new lawns throughout the summer. Established lawns rarely require watering. Even if they turn brown in summer they will soon recover following the first rains in autumn.

Lawn treatments Lawn weedkillers, moss killers and fertilizers can be applied any time the grass is growing strongly up until midsummer. If you intend to use more than one treatment, use a combined product.

Ponds

Plant up On a warm day in late spring or early summer plant up your pond or add new plants to an existing feature.

PLANT UP THE POND

Introduce new plants to the pond carefully. Flood the container with water and gently lower it to the appropriate depth.

Tidy ponds This is an ideal time to refurbish overgrown or neglected ponds. Blanketweed should be removed so that it does not develop into thick mats, which can entangle small fish. Clear excessive growth of blanketweed using a rake or bamboo cane and leave it on the side for a day or two to allow any trapped pond creatures to escape back into the water. Use a small net to remove duckweed. Divide and replant any overgrown plants.

Top up water During hot and windy spells keep the water levels topped up in ponds and in the reservoirs of all water features.

Propagate Now is a good time to propagate any plants that have become overgrown or if extra plants are needed.

Cut back Everything should be in full growth, particularly the oxygenators. Keep cutting these back so that the submerged shoots do not spread to the surface and become overgrown.

Pest and disease alert Pests such as blackfly and thrips on waterlily leaves can be jetted off with a strong hose.

Cut off Some sappy marginals, such as marsh marigolds (*Caltha palustris*), develop mildew in early summer. Cut off affected leaves completely; they will soon grow again.

This cottage garden, shown in early summer, is full of freshness and vitality as the borders begin to fill out with lush vegetation and flowers.

Feed fish Fish are very active now, but do not be tempted to overfeed. Feed little and often, and never with more than they can eat in five minutes.

Feed plants Slow-release pellets or sachets of fertilizer are sold for aquatics, particularly waterlilies. Push these just under the surface of the potting mix.

Check pond pumps The meshes on submersible pumps will clog quickly if there is any blanketweed that has accumulated near the pump. It is important to check the pump regularly and to keep it clear because the blanketweed will reduce the efficiency of the pump.

Oxygenate water features If there are fish in the pool, keep the pump running for watercourses or fountains on hot nights in order to help maintain oxygen levels. If there is no pump in the pond, then spray the surface of the water with a hosepipe.

Introduce new plants Tender floating plants, such as water hyacinth (*Eichhornia*) and water lettuce (*Pistia*), can be introduced to add interest.

REMOVE BLANKETWEED

To clear water of blanketweed, insert a cane into the water and twist it to wind the weed around it, rather like candyfloss.

CLEAN POND PUMPS

Algae and blanketweed can soon build up on the intake of pumps. Clean strainers and inlet holes regularly.

Late summer techniques

Now is the time to enjoy the garden. Late summer is usually a time of hot, dry weather, when there is a natural lull in the garden, and the glorious results of spring and early summer sowing and planting will be evident. Beds and borders will be filled with colourful blooms. The chores of early autumn can easily wait until the holidays are over and the weather becomes cooler. Most of the work in this month involves watering and other routine maintenance tasks such as mowing and hoeing, as well as clipping hedges.

Beds and borders

Feed container plants Continue feeding container plants unless you have already added a slow-release fertilizer at planting time. Use a balanced feed for general use and a high-potash fertilizer, such as tomato feed, for flowering and fruiting plants.

Watering It is vital that you water containers daily throughout the summer months. In borders, concentrate on watering any new plants, which should not go short of water during their first growing season.

PROPAGATE TENDER PERENNIALS

Cut off a sideshoot just below a leaf joint, about 2.5–10cm (1–4in) long. Trim off the lower leaves and insert the cutting in a pot.

Deadhead flowers Remove faded blooms from repeat-flowering plants, such as roses. Deadhead early-flowering perennials and annual bedding where practical to encourage further flushes of blooms. Trim straggly pansies. Deadhead self-seeders such as forget-me-nots and campanulas to prevent them becoming a weed problem.

Pest watch Stay vigilant for the first signs of pest and disease attacks, especially aphids, which can attack plants all around the garden; take appropriate action promptly. Spray susceptible roses against blackspot, mildew and rust. Hand-pick any caterpillars and sawfly grubs.

CLEAR EDGING

Some edging plants, such as this poached egg plant, can spill out on to the lawn, causing bald patches. Remove completely or trim back.

Save seed Collect seed from plants that you want to propagate. Cover the flower heads with paper bags and cut off when ripe.

Cut back shrubs Prune summer-flowering shrubs as soon as the display is over. Cut back fast-growing climbers, such as climbing and rambler roses. Pick lavender for drying.

Hedges Clip beech, holly, hornbeam and yew hedges, and most evergreen hedges, if you have not already done so earlier in the year.

Catalogues Order bulb catalogues and bulbs for autumn delivery.

Plant bulbs Plant autumn-flowering bulbs, such as sternbergia, in midsummer and spring-flowering bulbs in late summer.

Plant containers As summer flowers come to an end, begin planting up containers for autumn and winter displays.

Sow hardy annuals During late summer sow hardy annuals, such as calendula, candytuft and nigella, in prepared soil in the garden. During cold spells over winter, protect these with cloches or a double layer of garden fleece in cold areas.

Transplanting Polyanthus seedlings can be transplanted into their flowering positions in beds and borders.

Prune rambling roses such as *Rosa* 'Bobbie James' as soon as flowering has finished in late summer. This allows plenty of time for shoots to grow, ready for next season's crop of flowers.

Weed control Hoe beds and borders on a regular basis to keep down weeds.
Dahlias Feed and disbud dahlias and chrysanthemums as necessary.
Layering Border carnations can be propagated by layering.
Renovate borders Annuals and bedding plants that have finished flowering can be pulled up and added to the compost heap.

Lawns

Keep mowing Mow when necessary, and during dry spells raise the cutting height of your mower.
Watering lawns Water new lawns throughout the summer. Established lawns should not require watering. Even if they turn brown in summer, they will soon recover following the first rains in autumn.
Lawn treatments Lawn weedkillers, moss killers and fertilizers can be applied if the grass is growing strongly, up to midsummer. Use a combined product if necessary.

Garden Maintenance

Hard landscaping care Paths and drives should be kept weed-free by hand or by using a weedkiller.
Outdoor furniture At the end of the summer, most garden furniture will need to be put away in a garage or shed. The only types of furniture

TIE IN PLANTS

Keep an eye on plants that need support, such as tomatoes, and tie them in when necessary.

This garden, a riot of colour, shapes and textures, looks its best at the height of summer.

that are really frost- and rain-proof are non-folding items made from moulded resin, hardwood or cast aluminium. Before putting away the items, you may need to treat the furniture; the treatment depends on the material. Hardwoods, such as teak or iroko, should be treated with teak oil, while a preservative containing a fungicide should be applied every few years to softwoods.

Ponds

Top up water During hot and windy spells keep the water levels topped up in ponds and in the reservoirs of water features. If the water level drops, take the opportunity to check for cracks in concrete pools and preformed units or tears in flexible liners.
Oxygenate the water If fish are gulping at the surface of the pond in close, thundery weather, turn on the fountain or direct a jet of water from the hose into the water to churn the surface and help oxygenate the water.
Deadhead aquatics Remove faded blooms from repeat-flowering marginal plants and from bog garden plants.
Thin plants Overcrowded water lily pads can be thinned out, as can overgrown submerged plants.

Autumn and winter techniques

This is the time to prepare the garden for bad weather. In some areas quite severe frosts are common in early autumn, and in others light frosts may not occur until mid- or late autumn. Listen to the weather forecasts and take in or protect vulnerable plants if frost is expected. Consider some winter protection for plants on the borderline of hardiness, and be prepared to give early winter shelter, perhaps in the form of a windbreak, for newly planted evergreens. A little protection can ensure that many plants survive instead of succumbing to winter winds and cold. Make sure that all garden structures are sound and secure against wind and rain.

Beds and borders
Pot up tender perennials Tender perennials, such as pelargoniums, fuchsias and marguerites, should be lifted and potted up before the first frost to be overwintered in the greenhouse. If space is short, take cuttings instead.
Lift tender bulbs In colder areas, especially if the soil is heavy, tender bulbs such as gladioli should be lifted before the first frost and dried and stored somewhere frost-free. Check for rot every few weeks.

TIDY BORDERS

Clear summer bedding away and dig over the soil, removing large weeds. Rake the ground level so it looks neat and tidy.

Asters are one of the mainstays of the autumn garden. *Aster* x *frikartii* 'Mönch' flowers over a long period from summer to late autumn.

Plant bulbs There is still time to plant spring-flowering bulbs and winter containers.
Protect some shrubs Some shrubs are of borderline hardiness, depending on the area in which you live. It is important to protect vulnerable shrubs as well as hardy shrubs in exposed positions with a layer of windbreak netting lined with garden fleece, held taut between sturdy posts.

PROTECT CONTAINERS

Protect vulnerable container-grown plants with a layer of insulation. Plastic bubble wrap is a good choice.

Tie in wall shrubs Check wall shrubs and tie in new growth as necessary. Protect not-so-hardy types such as ceanothus with a double layer of garden fleece. Tender shrubs and climbers will need an insulating layer of leaves or straw, held in place with fine-mesh netting.
Pruning Long whippy growth on roses in exposed sites should be cut back by about one-third to prevent wind-rock loosening the roots. Winter prune wisteria. Cut back all stems of any Group 3 clematis (those that flower late in the season on the current year's growth, and herbaceous types).
New plants The dormant season is an ideal time to plant bare-rooted trees, shrubs and hedging plants.
Protect containers Leave only frost-proof containers outside in winter. Other containers, and the tender plants growing in them, may need protecting in colder areas. Wrap pots with bubble polythene to prevent the compost (soil mix) freezing solid. Protect the plant in a double layer of garden fleece. Leave a space for evergreen plants to be watered.
Wrap conifers Protect conifer specimens from being splayed open by heavy falls of snow by wrapping fine-mesh netting or a piece of thick soft string around them. Conifer hedges should have accumulations of snow knocked off before they cause damage to the branches.
Check stakes and ties Most climbers and many trees will have ties holding them on to a support or stake. Check these in winter to ensure they are secure but not too constricting.
Protect rock plants Excessive winter wet can damage plants with woolly foliage, such as those found in the rock garden. Protect by covering them with an open-ended cloche or a sheet of glass held up on bricks.

Clear summer bedding Remove annual plants from the border and dig over the ground ready for planting in the spring.

Lawns

Lawn repairs Early autumn is the perfect time to carry out maintenance tasks such as spiking and scarifying as well as essential lawn repairs.

Final cut Make the final cut once the grass has stopped growing. Then clean and service the lawn equipment before storage.

Fallen leaves Clear fallen leaves from the lawn through autumn and early winter so they do not smother the grass. Do not walk on the lawn if it is very wet or frosted.

Ponds

Fallen leaves Keep fallen leaves out of ponds by covering the feature with a lightweight fine-mesh netting. Clear any leaves collected in the netting regularly to prevent them rotting and fouling the water.

Autumn tidy up Cut back marginal plants, but take care not to cut those with hollow stems too short – the cut stems should remain proud of the water surface all winter.

Prevent freezing If the winter is severe, ice can be a problem if it covers the pool for prolonged periods. Methane gas, which is given off by decomposing vegetation, forms under the surface of the ice instead of being released to the atmosphere, and, because it is unable to escape, the methane is reabsorbed by the water, which becomes toxic to the fish. Use an electric heater to keep a small circle of the pool's surface free from ice. Alternatively, place a hot pan on the ice until it melts a hole and repeat this daily until the ice thaws. Never break the

ice by smashing through with a hammer, as this causes shock waves in the water that can damage the torpid fish.

Thick ice The expansion of thick ice can damage the sides of the pool. A pool with vertical side walls is more likely to be damaged than one with sloping sides. Placing objects such as spongy balls or pieces of wood in the water helps to absorb the pressure.

Move the pump If the pump is still operating a watercourse, lift it from the bottom so that it circulates colder water near the surface and does not disturb the beneficial layer of warmer water at the bottom of the pool.

Fish care If spells of mild weather trigger activity by the fish do not be tempted to feed them.

Dealing with snow Brush any snow off the ice in order to allow light into the pool.

Topping up If there are long periods of drying winds that cause the level

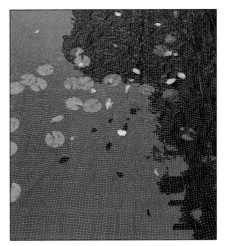

At the first signs of autumn leaf fall, suspend a fine plastic net over the pond surface to prevent leaves sinking into the water.

of the pool to drop, it is as important to top up in these periods as it is in the summer.

Protect waterlilies The dwarfer forms of waterlily may be damaged by severe cold in shallow pools. Remove them to a frost-free container full of water until the weather improves.

Prunus x subhirtella 'Stellata' has star-like pale pink flowers. It is an eye-catching feature in winter, flowering from late autumn to early spring, a time when the rest of the garden can appear dead.

Index

Page references in *italics* refer to illustrations.

A

acid soils 35
aphids 81
aquatic plants 57, 60–61, *60, 61,
    62*
arches 30–1, *30–1*
assessment
    gardens 10–11
    soil 34–5
Aster × frikartii 'Mönch' *92*
automatic watering 78, *79*
autumn techniques 92–3

B

beds
    autumn/winter jobs 92–3
    early summer jobs 88
    late summer jobs 90–1
    planning 20–3, *20–3*
    raised 22–3, *22, 23*
    spring jobs 86
blocks, laying *25, 27*
bog gardens 55, 64–5, *64, 65*
bonding, bricks 26, *26*
bonemeal, safety 83
borders
    autumn/winter jobs 92–3
    early summer jobs 88
    herbaceous 7
    late summer jobs 90–1
    planning 20–1
    spring jobs 86
    weeding 73
boundaries 26, 28–9
bricks *25,* 26, *26, 27, 27*
building
    fences 28–9, *28, 29*
    patios 16–17, *16, 17*
    ponds 58
    rock gardens 66–7
    structures 30–1, *30, 31*

walls 26–7, *26, 27*
    see also planning
bulbs 52

C

caterpillars 81, *81*
Chamaemelum nobile 14
circles, marking out *20*
Clematis
    C. 'Lady Betty Balfour' *70*
    C. 'Prince Charles' *17*
climbers 31
cloches *87*
columbines 7
compost 38–9
crevices 26
cultivators 37
cutting tools *70*

D

decking 15, 18–19, *18–19*
designing *see* planning
Dictamnus albus (dittany) *73*
digging
    lawns 44–5

Rosa x *alba* 'Alba Semiplena'

tools 70, *70*
    types 36–7, *36, 37*
dividing 74, *74*
double digging *36, 37*
drainage, lawns 48
drawings, plans 12–13

E

edging
    lawns 48–9, *49, 50, 51, 51*
    paths 25, *25*
    ponds 58, 59, *59*
English bond 26
Erysimum 80

F

feeding *see* fertilizers
fertilizers 40–1
    compost 38–9
    lawns 47
    techniques 79, *79*
fish, feeding *87*
Flemish bond 26
foliar feeding 41
foundations 26

G

garden structures 30–1
grass cuttings 76, *76*
gravel 15, *15*
greenhouses *10*
ground cover *14,* 15, 74–5, *74, 75*
ground preparation 21, *21*

H

hedges 82
herbs, lawns 14
Hypericum calycinum 15, 74

I

illusion of space 20
inorganic fertilizers 41, *41*
inorganic mulches 76–7, *77*
Iris sibirica 55

Narcissus 'Tête-à-tête'

Acknowledgements

The publisher would like to thank all the garden owners, designers and institutions who kindly allowed photography in their gardens, especially Bosvigo House, Cornwall (1, 5br); East Ruston Old Vicarage, Norfolk (2, 96/designers Alan Gray and Graham Robeson); RHS Hampton Court Flower Show 2001 (4bl/designer Mark Davis); Butterstream, Ireland (4br/designer Jim Reynolds); RHS Tatton Park Flower Show 2001 (5tl).

The publisher would like to thank Peter McHoy for his permission to use the following photographs:
14t; 18bl, bc and br; 19bl, bc and br; 45b; 58 bl, bc and br; 59bl, bc and br

Photography: Peter Anderson, Jonathan Buckley, Paul Forrester, John Freeman, Michelle Garrett, Janine Hosegood, Andrea Jones, Simon McBride, Marie O'Hara and Steve Wooster

Illustrations: Neil Bulpitt, Liz Pepperell, Michael Shoebridge

Additional step-by-step text: Peter McHoy, Richard Bird, Andrew Mikolajski, Ted Collins, Blaise Cooke, Christopher Grey-Wilson, Lin Hawthorne, Jessica Houdret, Hazel Key, Peter Robinson, Susie White

A formal garden with box balls.